The Antipodean

Cookery Book

AND

KITCHEN COMPANION

BY

Mrs. LANCE RAWSON

Author of "The Queensland Cookery Book", "The Australian Poultry Book" and "The Australian Enquiry Book"

Kangaroo Press

First published in 1895 by George Robertson and Company
This facsimile edition published in 1992 by Kangaroo Press Pty Ltd
3 Whitehall Road (P.O. Box 75) Kenthurst NSW 2156
Printed by Star Printery Pty Ltd, Erskineville 2043

ISBN 0 86417 454 3

PREFACE

Once more I come before my sister housewives with a cheap and useful little work on cookery, adapted and written expressly to meet the wants and circumstances of those living in the far Bush, as well as those who dwell within reach of the amenities of civilized existence.

The fact that my other works have met with a most generous welcome from housekeepers, poultry farmers, etc., etc., all over Australia will, I trust, ensure a like reception for this, my latest effort.

That "The Australian Inquiry Book," published barely a year ago, should be already in its second edition is most encouraging, and leads me to hope for as great a success for "The Antipodean Cookery Book and Kitchen Companion."

(MRS.) LANCE RAWSON.

Rockhampton,
February 11th, 1895.

The Antipodean Cookery Book

Advice and Suggestions for the Housewife.

SOME twenty years ago Owen Meredith said in one of his novels, when describing the loves of two extremely blue-blooded young people, "We may live without friends, we may live without books, but civilized man cannot live without his cook." And what was said then is just as true to-day. Man must be cooked for. He'll do without shirt-buttons, and he'll do without his slippers, but he will not do without his dinner, nor is he inclined to accept excuses as regards under- or over-done meals after the first week or so of the honeymoon. If there be any young girls reading these pages who are contemplating marriage in the near future, take an old wife's advice and learn to cook, for only by feeding him well will you succeed in gaining your husband's respect and keeping his affection. The husband is a creature of appetite, believe me, and not to be approached upon any important matter, such as a new bonnet or a silk dress, on an empty stomach.

And I think the husband is right. Nowadays all the arrangements and appliances for cooking are so good that the wife who cannot cook or show her servant how to has neglected her opportunities. See the stoves in use now and the numerous utensils and labour-saving machines with which almost every kitchen is furnished. When I look at the old-fashioned camp-oven and the cross-handled chopper for mincing meat I often think the wives of those times served a martyrdom, and I believe they did just as much, if not more, cooking than we do, with our natty little American or gas stoves and our useful mincing-machines. One great art in cooking, especially in the Bush, consists in making the best of poor materials, and in utilizing whatever we find ready to our hands, and in being able to use any oven or fireplace, even an open fire on the ground, with the ashes in which to cook the damper. Nowadays one is seldom called upon to cook by such primitive means, unless when camping out, or newly married, and in a strange land. I add the last because I have the liveliest recollection of the first meal I cooked for my husband, or attempted to cook, I should say, for matters ended in his taking things into his own hands, while I retired to weep and recover from the effects of the smoke.

Let me suggest to prospective brides that they should stipulate for a stove if marrying a Bushman. A man will promise anything before marriage, very little after. I was wise in my generation, and stipulated for a *stove* and a mangle in preference to a piano, and got all three. In the Bush, where servants come and go like angels' visits, the housewife finds the benefit of the many labour-saving machines now in existence. I can speak from a personal experience of many of them, and can assure my readers that a lady—no matter how unaccustomed to work, provided she be willing to do it—can do the whole of her housework with very little exertion or fatigue to herself if she has the following machines :—

1. A washing-machine.
2. A wringer.
3. A mincing-machine.
4. A knife-cleaning machine.
5. Small kerosene stove.
6. Patent egg-beater.
7. Scrubbing - brush with long handle.
8. A brass box iron.
9. A mangle.
10. A good American stove.
11. A chain pot-cleaner.

Some of these may not come under the heading of exactly labour-saving machines, though they really are such.

Of washing-machines there are several in the market—some very costly and complicated. I have used "The Walton," which is an excellent machine for a large family; but of all these machines I prefer the small tin funnel made with a concave foot to fit the boiler, and which cleanses by suction, the water being drawn down, then sucked through the funnel to the top, and discharged over the clothes again. Of the three or four washing-machines I have used, that one gave most satisfaction, and the cost is so trifling that it is within the reach of every housewife. Any tin-smith would make one for 3s. or 4s.

The wringer is almost a necessity to a woman whose wrists are weak, or who has not been used to doing the washing. They are not expensive, and if properly used and cared for will last for years. They must not be left in the sun when done with, and should be well dried after using. The small standard mangle can be used as a wringer, but it is false economy, in my opinion, as the wooden rollers soon get dented and roughened.

With a mangle the first expense is the last, as it will last a lifetime, and will save the housewife an immensity of trouble. For my own part, I prefer all children's clothes and my own morning dresses and wrappers put through the mangle when it falls to myself to do the ironing of the same. Table linen lasts clean twice as long if put through the mangle every day.

A good box iron is invaluable to the housewife whose time is required for other things besides ironing. I would not advise their being entrusted to the ordinary Bush domestic, or indeed to any one save the mistress or daughters of the house, because they must be kept spotlessly clean and free from rust. They are a saving in both time and fuel, the charcoal for them being easily collected about the paddock wherever a log or stump has been burnt out.

A mincing-machine is about the most useful thing in a kitchen. By it bread crumbs can be made in a few minutes, suet chopped, and meat of all kinds can be used when put through it. When bread crumbs are made—if for cutlets, or for anything requiring them fine—sift through a hair-sieve, and you will get them just right. They are sometimes the better for being put through twice, and suet should always be put through two, or even three times.

A knife-cleaning machine is, of course, not a necessary, but every housewife who does her own work knows the constant and wearying trouble of cleaning the knives. There is a very nice little machine that screws on to the table, having two rollers, like a wringer. I had one for years, and found it a great comfort ; but I do not remember the maker's name.

A kerosene stove. This is useful to the woman who does her own work, because if she comes home tired, or disinclined to trouble with the preparation of an elaborate meal, she can boil water for tea, and cook a small dish or two if necessary. Also it is useful in the Bush, where the men must have breakfast at sun up or before ; and for afternoon tea, in the case of visitors whom she does not wish to leave, she can light the lamp, and have her water boiling in a few minutes.

A patent egg-beater is merely optional ; for my own part, I much prefer a fork.

Scrubbing-brush with long handle. These are very useful, and save one many a backache and sore knee ; but they are nearly useless without a mop or drier of some sort. The long handles are sold (and can be fitted to any brush) having a clamp, and with them a room can be scrubbed out without ever going down on the knees. A mop is easily made of strips of old flannel, or, what I found better still, a round, soft ball stuffed with flannel pieces, and which can be so used that it soaks up the wet quicker and cleaner than the ragged mop.

I need say very little about stoves. There are so many good ones in the market that it would not be fair, even if possible, to make comparisons.

A "chain pot-cleaner" is most useful, and if it be fixed on to a handle, the hands need not be even soiled.

Enamel saucepans, frying-pans, etc., are far before the ordinary iron for the housewife who is her own servant; they are easier to clean and so much pleasanter to use.

Elsewhere I have given a recipe for a good washing mixture, which will be a great help to the young housewife doing her own washing. For moleskin trousers let me advise the use of a soft scrubbing-brush. Lay the leg of the trousers out straight on the washing-bench, and scrub it with the brush and plenty of soap. Then when the whole has gone through this process, rinse in clean water, and *then* put into the boiler. This rinsing before boiling makes a wonderful difference to their colour ; by it all the dirty water is taken out before they are boiled. If you have the washing-funnel they only need packing round it and the ordinary soap and soda added to the water, but if you have no funnel, and the moles are very dirty, a teaspoonful of ammonia added to the boiler will make all the difference in the world. Ammonia is the most useful chemical you can have in the laundry kitchen, or pantry. All obstinate stains, or indeed stained linen, table-cloths, sheets, pillow-cases, etc., etc., if soaked in water to which ammonia has been added will come back to their normal colour. I find it the only thing that will take out the yellow stain of perspiration from pillow-cases and gentlemen's underwear. To the young beginner in laundry work I would say, Be careful not to rub your knuckles instead of the clothes ; get some old hand to show you or watch her washing. Having suffered in this way myself, I would like to spare others. The board also requires to be seen in use, or the tips and nails of the fingers suffer. Turn all socks and stockings on the wrong side before soaking ; wash them, turn and wash again, and turn to rinse. After boiling everything should be blued on the wrong side. If table-linen is starched, add the starch to the blue-water, or make what is called water-starch, which is merely the blue-water slightly thickened. All black prints should be rinsed in salt and water, to prevent the dye running. For blues, purples, and all delicate colours of those tints, a little sugar of lead in the water will set the colours.

Alum will set greens. But all delicate colours should be washed out quickly in cold water if possible, and dried in the shade, so the sun will not fade them. For French muslins, Indian muslins, etc., wash in water in which a small bag of bran has been boiled. Then if dried quickly and ironed they will have the appearance of new material ; the bran gives a gloss and just the required stiffness.

For very dirty towels and kitchen cloths a tablespoonful of kerosene in the boiler will bring out the dirt. Where the housewife is her own servant she will be wise to have sufficient kitchen cloths and towels to be able to put them into her general weekly or fortnightly wash. If she is careful four tea-towels, two glass ditto, and two rough cloths per week will be ample. The tidy housewife will require several aprons for the different work she has to do.

For scrubbing and cleaning nothing is better than a three-bushel bag cut open, and two strings fastened to it to tie it round the waist; it wants no making beyond that. A pair of very big sleeves are most useful to protect the dress sleeves. They can be made of almost any material. It takes about a yard for each, and the cuff part is gathered into a band to fit the wrist, and buttoned, or what I find better than a button, is a piece of elastic run through. At the shoulder, or upper arm, use another elastic or a tape to pin to the neck of the dress. With a pair of these sleeves and a wide apron one can undertake any work without soiling one's dress. I have lately received a pattern of a housewife's "overall" from a lady who saw them used in Germany. It is simply a wide over-gown that covers the dress, and with wide sleeves and tight-fitting cuffs; a cord runs through at the waist to draw it in. It is merely a matter of opinion which is best; where washing is a consideration, I should say the apron and sleeves.

For washing a coarse apron lined with a piece of water-proof sheeting is what is generally used; but I much prefer one with a high bib, and shaped off at the sides, so as to reach far round the skirt, and made of black American cloth. There is a child's pinafore the exact shape; indeed, it was from this I got the idea. It is cut all in one piece, bib and all, but requires binding, and can then be fastened with buttons and loops at the neck, and low at the back of the skirt. Any one who has ever seen Madame Weigal's patterns will know the pinafore I mean. I think it has a pocket across the front. From two to two and a half yards of American cloth will cut one for a tall woman. Mine lasted over eighteen months, washing in it every week, and sometimes oftener; so it was not expensive. I paid 1s. 3d. per yard for the cloth, but it can be got cheaper. For ordinary kitchen aprons nothing is better than the dowlas used for kitchen towels. I adopted the somewhat novel plan of making most of my tea-towels into aprons (through having got into the habit of picking up my apron to wipe everything), and I found that I saved time by it, for it is often quicker to dry with one's apron than the towel one has laid down somewhere. Several ladies to whom I told this plan at once adopted it, and were pleased with it. One can always change the damp apron for a dry one when necessary. When one has to go down on the knees to scrub, it is *actually necessary* to have some sort of pad or cushion. I found the latter a nuisance, on account of having to move it so often, and I tried padding the bottom part of my apron. This answered fairly well and satisfied me, until I hit upon the idea of making separate pads for my knees, and with which I no longer dreaded scrubbing-day. I made them of sawdust, in strong covers. It will not do to have it in *one* cushion, as with the weight of the knee the thickness gets all to one side ; but make about three casings, and stuff all. I think rags would do as well, or perhaps better, than sawdust. The pads should be cut to fit the bend of the knee, short at the sides, long in the middle. When going to scrub tie them on, and I can assure any housewife that she will be able to scrub three rooms with less pain and trouble, and in less time, than she would one without them.

Many housewives wear gloves to work in. It is hardly necessary if they have a little washing-up mop made of flannel. You require two or three of them to have things nice. One for washing all the teacups and silver things that are not greasy, another for dinner-plates and greasy things, and a third for the rougher work of pans, saucepans, etc., etc. If the man of the house is at all handy at carpentering, the housewife can save herself endless trouble if she will get him to make her a square portable rack for the greasy dinner-plates. I made mine myself, but it was very rough and primitive, and was merely an open sort of box, into which I used to pack the dirty plates and dishes, and standing it in the washing-up tub, pour the hot soapsuds over. I had a strong handle to it, and so could lift it up and down to souse it, and get the plates clean. Then from this I stood it in a large milk-dish, and with a gardener's watering-can rinsed them well with cold water. This idea could be improved on with a well-made rack. Before I hit on this mode of washing up, I had another, which consisted in boiling the plates. I cup open a kerosene tin lengthways, and when this was filled with soapy water, with soda or a few drops of ammonia, added to it, and on the fire, I put my greasy plates in directly it was boiling, left them a few moments, and then removed to the rack to dry. I have the greatest objection to washing greasy things, hence my many inventions and contrivances. Nothing is more useful than a plate-rack, as plates can thus be dried without the aid of a cloth, and they are never sticky if properly washed. The washing fluid I have given elsewhere is capital for washing up.

To clean greasy frying-pans a small lump of soda or a few drops of ammonia in the water is usually effectual.

The best way with saucepans, stewpans, etc., is to put them into a kerosene tin and boil them well; all not too large can be treated in this way, and it saves endless work. Once the housewife gets her kitchen thoroughly clean and shipshape, it very seldom gets beyond her again.

The heart-breaking time is when she has to take it over from a dirty or careless servant, who has left her everything, from her kitchen tables to the lamps, in a state of grime and filth. When tables are really past recovery there are only three alternatives—viz., planing afresh, painting, or covering with American cloth. Let me warn the housewife against enamelling. I once tried it, with most unsatisfactory result. If not too bad, a few applications of bath-brick, kerosene, and soap and water will have a good effect, or oxalic acid, I believe, will whiten wood. An old dresser looks very well if stained and varnished, and if the housewife wishes to really have a pretty or artistic kitchen, she can stain and varnish a border round the floor, and have a square of linoleum or oil-cloth in the centre.

All pot lids once cleaned and brightened, or that have never lost their colour, can be kept in proper order and condition if boiled once a week in a kerosene tin of soapsuds, two table-spoonfuls of whiting, and one of ammonia. Let them boil for an hour, remove the tin from the fire, and when cold take out the lids, dry them well, and polish with the leather. There should be two chamois leathers, one for silver and glass, the other for the tins, pot-lids, etc. They can be washed and will last a long time. A recipe is given for washing them in the Household Recipes.

The burners of all kerosene lamps should be boiled once a month in soap and soda water. Very often when the lamps (after a time) begin to burn badly, without apparent cause, it is the wick that is to blame, water seems to get into it and cause trouble. The remedy is to substitute a fresh wick for a day or two, and boil the one taken out in water and a few drops of ammonia ; dry it in the sun, and it will be good as new again. When washing lamp glasses rinse in vinegar and water, and the flies will not spot them so readily. Windows can be treated the same way.

Half a dozen pot and iron holders are not too many in a kitchen ; the legs of old tweed and mole-skin trousers make excellent holders. Cut into lengths, pad with any scraps, and then sew across and across in the machine, bind round the edges, and put a loop of tape to hang by.

The square tops cut from kerosene tins, when the latter become buckets, make very good stands for saucepans, stewpans, etc., on the kitchen table ; they should be hung up in a handy place and within easy reach.

The housewife should keep a small slate always in the kitchen, particularly if she is in the Bush, or far from a town, and where supplies can only be got out at certain times, as then she can jot down things wanted when she thinks of them.

I saw an excellent idea in a friend's kitchen some little time ago. For the benefit of her servants she had written out all the recipes for their favourite puddings, cakes, etc., and a few special dishes of meat, and these were tacked up behind the door. And in another place she had the days of the week, with the duties for each day. It struck me as a capital idea for the housewife doing her own work. In the first case of the recipes, one often is puzzled for a moment to know what to make, and would perhaps not recall to mind some recipes till it was too late, whereas if it were there handy one would be grateful ; and as regards the daily duties, the list would act as a good reminder very often.

Hints for the Household.

Keep a saucer of unslaked lime in the cupboard or pantry to absorb all damp.

Newspapers are the best polishers for windows and lamp chimneys.

Ammonia will dissolve grease. Always keep a bottle in the kitchen.

Potato skins rubbed on the hands will take away the smell of onions.

Rinse saucepans that have boiled onions in raw potato water.

Lemon juice may be kept a long time if strained into small bottles and about a teaspoonful of salad oil added on top. Cork and keep dry.

Stuff fowls in the breast where the crop has been taken out; they look better and the stuffing is more easily got at. Bread sauce is one of the nicest additions to roast fowl.

Jerusalem artichokes are cooked just the same as potatoes, peeled, washed, and put into cold water to boil twenty minutes, counting from when the water begins to boil. They are usually served with melted butter poured over them.

Cut up parsley with a pair of scissors.

Thyme and sage should be dried in the oven till they can be powdered in the hand. Three or four minutes in a hot oven or on top of the stove will do it.

Keep the green celery leaves, wash them, and dry on a plate in the oven. They will do to flavour soups, stews, etc., when celery is not in season.

When blending flour mix with very little milk at first, stir into a paste, and then gradually add more liquid till it is the right consistency.

Custard will curdle if you pour the eggs into the boiling milk, but not if you pour the milk on to the eggs very slowly and keep stirring a minute or two.

Suet may be kept in a jar covered with a weak brine.

Copper skewers with large iron heads will hasten the cooking of a joint, and are much used in households where the meat is liked well cooked. The iron head absorbs the heat and conducts it by means of the copper wire into the centre of the meat, and thus enables it to be cooked simultaneously with the outer portions. Any blacksmith or tinsmith would make these skewers.

It is usual to serve either ham, bacon, or tongue with roast fowls or turkeys.

FREEZING MIXTURES.—One pound of ice, broken up, and half a pound of saltpetre mixed with one pint of cold water. —Twelve ounces of sal-ammoniac and eight ounces of saltpetre dissolved in one pint of boiling water and allowed to get cold.—Half a pound of salt to one pound of ice, broken up, one pint cold water.—These are all freezing mixtures that might be used on special occasions to freeze puddings, etc., etc., when one cannot go to the expense of more elaborate freezers or when one has no ice chest. All things to be frozen must be immersed to the edge of the mould in the mixture.

Housekeeping Economies.

The young wife about to establish a home should not lay out all her money at once. She will find endless enjoyment and satisfaction in buying here and there, as the need arises for certain pieces of furniture, or as she finds a place for them. Such a home soon becomes a collection of household treasures, each article or piece having its own little history, and thus acquiring a meaning and value far deeper than the longest purse could purchase.

The careful housewife takes note of the kitchen fire. If using a stove, she closes up the dampers when not requiring the fire, and thus saves her fuel.

She saves all her drippings and the skimming from the soup pot, clarifies them, and makes them serve in place of butter for cakes, sauces, pastry, etc.

She saves all scraps of bread and meat left over from meals, and works them up into tasty little puddings and dishes.

Keeps old brooms for rough work, and so prolongs the lives of the best.

Uses up worn garments in making quilts, comforts, rag carpets, or rugs.

Polishes windows and lamp chimneys with old newspapers.

Rubs the copper out with a kerosene cloth before putting it away each week.

Paints the inside of tubs when they get too rusty to be of use without.

Always uses an apron in the kitchen, and when about house-work.

Keeps special clothes for very dirty work.

Turns the sheets when they grow thin in the middle.

Cuts up worn tablecloths for everyday napkins.

Keeps rugs spread over places in the carpet that are subjected to the hardest wear.

Thoroughly dries all tin ware, or it will rust into holes.

Cuts open the empty kerosene tins for use as buckets, boilers, fish kettles, etc.

Saves all waste fat and stale dripping to make soap.

Make dish-cloths out of old socks and stockings, split up and stitched together. Black stockings do as well as white.

When boiling fish always add a spoonful or two of vinegar, or the juice of a lemon, to the water; the acid helps to keep the fish firm.

Fish should always be fried in olive oil in preference to dripping.

Good beef-dripping may be used instead of butter for parsley and butter, onion sauce, etc., only one-third less should be allowed.

An apple added to sage and onion stuffing both adds to the flavour and prevents the onions repeating.

Sweetbreads must always be parboiled as soon as possible after they are taken from the animal. A little lemon juice added to the water will help to blanch them. Boil them from fifteen to twenty minutes.

For seasoning, the juice of the onion is often preferred to the whole. One teaspoonful extracted with the aid of a lemon squeezer is sufficient to flavour stuffing.

In bread sauce use onion juice in preference to chopped-up onion.

For salads, to impart the flavour of onions, rub the salad bowl with a piece of raw onion.

Hints on Boiling Fish.

To every two quarts of water allow one tablespoonful of salt and the same of vinegar; do not put fish into boiling water or it will crack the skin. It is only the deeply coloured fish that is put into boiling water to set the colour.

Things to keep by you.

A GLUE THAT RESISTS DAMP. — Put some glue into a bottle and fill up with whisky or acetic acid. Cork well till it is dissolved, when it will be fit to use.

TO STOP A LEAK IN THE WASH-UP DISH, ETC.—Mix whiting with common soap in equal quantities and rub into the hole.

Hints for the Kitchen.

To clean the table scrub well with soap and powdered bath brick. Monkey soap answers the same purpose, but is expensive. A bath brick will cost twopence, and can be used instead of Monkey soap for all purposes.

For washing-up have a kerosene tin of water with soap cut up and soda in it on the fire. Take out what you want into your wash-up dish, use a good dish-cloth and you will not require any more soap.

Porridge.—Soak the oatmeal over night in cold water, and it will then not require such long boiling.

Knife handles can be easily cleaned by the application of a little salts of lemon on a damp rag.

All cooking utensils, tops of lamps, etc., should be well boiled in strong soda-water and soap every three or four months.

To cleanse and sweeten your dish-cloth boil it in strong soap and soda-water, then rinse in plain hot water; do this once a week.

A GOOD GREASE ERADICATOR.—Boil one ounce of soap, cut small, in one quart of water; add one teaspoonful of saltpetre and one and a half ounces of ammonia. Bottle and keep well corked.

Cold boiled potatoes used like soap will thoroughly cleanse the hands and keep the skin soft.

To clean fat after frying, slice up a raw potato into it and cook for a few minutes; the potato seems to collect all impurities.

A good glue to have handy is made by soaking a piece of ordinary glue in water till it softens (not dissolves), then pour off the water and add linseed oil. Stand the jar or bottle in a saucepan of water over the fire till the glue has dissolved and it is the thickness of jelly. This glue may

B

be used for mending or joining all sorts of things, and it has the advantage of resisting water.

To wash kitchen cloths, give them a good rubbing on the board and put on to boil in water, to which there is added one tablespoonful of kerosene.

To preserve china and glassware from cracking, when new, put it into a boiler of cold water, in which about half a pound of salt is dissolved, and let it come to the boil gradually and boil for ten or fifteen minutes; then allow it to cool slowly. All tumblers, lamp chimneys, decanters, etc., should be treated in this way. They can be done in any large saucepan or a kerosene tin.

Hints for the Literary Worker.

The literary worker and all who lead a sedentary existence require almost special diet. Their food should be light and digestible at all times. Poultry, fish, eggs, succulent vegetables and fruit should form their chief diet.

If they work late at night, as they invariably do as a rule, they should have a cup of warm milk or some warm drink directly upon waking in the morning, and positively no work should be done until after breakfast.

The digestive organs being most active during the early portion of the day, a hearty meal should be eaten about noon, and a rest of an hour or two should follow before work is begun again. Part of the afternoon should be spent in the open air, and at night a light, digestible dinner might be partaken of. When night work is a regular and recognised thing food should be taken about midnight and again at 4 o'clock. Strong meats and drinks should be avoided at all times, and plenty of milk substituted, with eggs, fruit, fresh vegetables, and salads. The literary man or woman needs all his or her vital energy to keep up the supply necessary to their mental and physical strength.

The literary worker is seldom a large eater, therefore he requires what he does eat to be of the best and most strengthening.

Things to be Remembered.

That fried croutons are served with peasoup.

That apple sauce is served with roast goose and roast pork.

That red currant jelly is served with roast saddle of mutton.

That mint sauce is served with roast lamb.

That bread sauce is served with roast turkey and roast fowl.

That egg sauce is served with boiled fish.

That melted butter, or white sauce, is served with boiled fowls.

That caper sauce is served with boiled mutton, and sometimes onion sauce.

That onion sauce is served with boiled rabbit and boiled bandicoot.

That parsley sauce is often served with boiled mutton and boiled fish.

That melted butter is served with cauliflower, boiled onions, vegetable marrow, artichokes, boiled cucumber, broad beans, and boiled turnips.

That foam balls, nut balls, anchovy balls are served with soup.

That boiled rice and a small jug of cream are served with mullagatawny soup.

When frying or poaching eggs, first break them one at a time into a cup, and when transferring the egg to the pan submerge the rim of the cup in the boiling fat or water, and slip the egg very gently from it. By this means you avoid breaking the egg, and also keep the white from spreading and becoming ragged.

That brandy sauce, arrowroot, butter, or boiled custard, are served with plum pudding.

That wine sauce is served with sweet boiled puddings.

That jam and boiled custard are served with blanc mange.

That sweet white sauce is served with marmalade pudding and also rolly-poly.

That brandy sauce is served with plum pudding.

That arrowroot sauce is served with plum pudding.

Things to Know.

When roasting meat allow a quarter of an hour to each pound, and an extra half-hour to every eight pounds.

White meats, such as pork and veal, require a little longer.

Have a brisk fire for the first ten minutes (so as to close up the pores and keep the gravy in), then cook slowly. Baste constantly. About half a cup of hot water poured into the baking tin after the first fifteen minutes will improve the meat.

Soap.—*Ingredients :*—3 pounds washing soda, 3 pounds lime, 12 quarts water, 3 pounds fat, 4 ounces resin, or grass tree gum. *Mode :*—Mix the soda and lime in the water, and let them boil for about twenty minutes. Then remove from the fire and let the sediment settle. Pour off the lye and add the fat (clarified) to it, and the resin or gum. Let it boil slowly for two to nearly three hours. Then when cool pour into a prepared box, and when hard turn out and cut into bars.

For Stained Hands.—The housewife who is her own domestic, general servant, etc., etc., requires always to have handy something or other that will take stains and stickiness from the hands. For the purpose nothing is better than oxalic acid, but the housewife will do well to keep three bottles on her washstand—oxalic acid, and sal soda, in saturated solution, and a small bottle of pure alcohol. A saturated solution is made by putting the crystals or powder into the bottle, and then adding just sufficient water to cover it well. The water can only dissolve a certain amount of the acid, so that the solution is thus very strong, and two or three drops of this will remove almost any fruit or vegetable stain. Many persons fail in the use of the acid because they do not apply it properly. It must be rubbed on when the hands have been washed as clean as possible without soap. Wait a few moments for it to take effect, rubbing it meanwhile with the fingers or a nail-brush, then rinse thoroughly in clear water.

The solution of sal soda will remove all taint and trace of grease from the hands. Gums like varnish and some kinds of paint are best removed by the use of a few drops of alcohol.

It is a very easy matter to keep the hands in good condition with a little pains taken after every washing of them. A few drops of glycerine or a tiny scrap of honey will prevent roughness and chapping and save the hands considerably.

Marble Cake.—FOR THE WHITE CAKE.—*Ingredients:* 1 cup butter, 3 cups white sugar, 5 cups flour (even), ½ cup sweet milk, ½ teaspoon soda, whites of 8 eggs, lemon flavouring

For the Dark Cake.—*Ingredients :* 1 cup butter, 2 cups brown sugar, 1 cup molasses, 1 cup sour milk, 1 teaspoon soda, 4 cups flour, yolks of 8 eggs, and 1 whole egg, spices of all sorts, according to taste. *Mode :* Having mixed both cakes pretty firmly, put a layer of dark into the tin, then a layer of light, and so on, finishing with a layer of dark. Bake in a hot oven.

This quantity makes a very large, but an excellent cake for a children's tea-party or for afternoon tea. It can be iced if preferred.

For a Weak Chest.—*Ingredients :* ½ pint of whisky, ½ pound golden syrup, 1 ounce pure glycerine. *Mode :* Mix these ingredients thoroughly, pour into a bottle, and take a tablespoonful two or three times a day.

Scones.—*Ingredients :* 1 pound flour, ½ teaspoon salt, ½ teaspoon baking soda (well crushed), 1 cupful or a little more thick or well soured milk. *Mode :* Sift the flour, add the salt and the soda, well crushed with a knife blade, mix thoroughly, then make a hole in the centre and stir in the thick milk, work into a dough, roll out and cut into scones about half an inch thick. Bake in a very quick oven. Butter may be added if liked.

Pressed Chicken.—Good picnic dish.—*Ingredients :* 3 or 4 chickens, 1 tablespoonful isinglass to each 3 or 4 pounds of chicken, pepper and salt. *Mode :* Boil the chickens in a little water until very tender, so that the flesh will separate from the bones. Cut the meat up very fine, season it with pepper and salt. Add to the liquor in which it was boiled a tablespoonful of isinglass, keep stirring till it is dissolved. Place the chicken in a deep dish or basin, pour the liquor over it, put a weight on top, and when cold turn out.

Very Good Plain Dumpling. — *Ingredients :* 2 cups flour, 1 teaspoonful salt, ½ teaspoon soda, ½ cup chopped suet, 1 cup butter milk, or sour milk. *Mode :* Mix the salt and soda with the flour, rub in the suet, and then stir in the butter milk. It may require a little more or less flour, as some flour thickens more than others. The paste should be just stiff enough to stir easily. Drop pieces into a greased steamer, and steam three-quarters of an hour.

To Make French Rolls.—*Ingredients :* 4 potatoes of medium size, yeast, 1 quart flour, salt. *Mode :* Peel and boil the potatoes and mash them up fine in the water in which they were boiled. Stir them into a quart of flour, adding the usual quantity of yeast. Make the dough thick and hard so it will hold together, as in rising it softens so much that it can be kneaded without sticking. The kneading is most important. A quarter of an hour ought to suffice for a small recipe like the one given.

Knead by drawing out one end like a rope and coiling the other portion over and over. Another object of making the dough thick and stiff to begin with is to avoid putting in flour after the dough is light, for the potatoes soften so much that it will be just right when fermented.

After the kneading stand it to rise again, and when light knead as before. A third working will improve, but is not necessary. Cut each roll out of the mass of dough, shape as lightly and quickly as possible, place them in the baking tin about an inch apart. Let them stand five or six minutes, then put into the oven, and ten minutes should bake them.

When half done moisten the tops with a feather dipped in milk.

Good rolls ought to be puffs of flour ; they should tear in shreds or strips with a fibre or grain like the husk of a cocoanut.

To Detect the Adulteration of Milk.—Take a long slender bottle thoroughly cleaned and dry. Fill with the suspected milk, and stand in a cool (not cold) place for forty-eight hours, when all foreign fluid will be precipitated. The sour milk will fill the middle of the bottle, and the fatty substance will float on the top. Sometimes there will be a layer of cream, then a layer of albumen, an artificial device to make the milk look rich ; then will come the soured milk, and at the bottom will be the foreign water.

A Lenten Pudding.—*Ingredients :* 3 ounces ground rice, 1½ pint milk, 3 ounces butter, 4 ounces sugar, 4 eggs, a pinch of salt, grated rind of $\frac{1}{2}$ a lemon, a little puff paste, $\frac{1}{2}$ a cup of sultanas or currants. *Mode:* Mix the ground rice with half the milk or a little less, and put the rest of the milk on to boil in an enamelled saucepan. When it boils stir in the rice and boil for fifteen minutes. Remove from the fire and beat in the butter and sugar. Break the eggs into a basin, whisk them well, add a pinch of salt, the grated lemon rind, and then pour the contents of the saucepan over them and mix well. When this is nearly cold, have a deep pie dish lined with puff paste, and pour it into it. Strew the top with well washed sultanas or currants, and bake for fifteen or twenty minutes in a gentle oven

Gingerbread.—*Ingredients:* 3 ounces moist sugar, 2 eggs, $\frac{1}{2}$ pound good treacle, $\frac{1}{2}$ pound flour, $\frac{1}{2}$ ounce ginger, $\frac{1}{2}$ teaspoonful powdered cloves, grated rind of 1 lemon. *Mode:* Whisk the eggs to a froth, and pour on them by degrees the $\frac{1}{2}$ pound of treacle, beating well all the time. Add the sugar in the same way and the flour. Oil the butter before the fire or in the oven, and pour it in a little at a time, beating the mixture till all is in. Everything depends on the mixing being well done. No butter should appear on the surface, and the ingredients should be so well whisked that large bubbles should appear in it to the last. Add the ginger, cloves, and lemon rind (grated). Butter a shallow tin, pour in the gingerbread and bake in a moderate oven. When done let it cool before turning out. Time to bake, from three-quarters to an hour.

Lentils.—*Ingredients:* Lentils (about a breakfast cupful), 1 tablespoonful butter, pepper, salt, 1 teaspoonful vinegar, 1 tablespoonful chopped parsley. *Mode:* Soak the lentils over night in some cold water. Next morning drain them and throw them into a quart or so of boiling water. Let them boil for half an hour or till tender, but not broken. Strain away the water, add the butter to the lentils, the pepper, salt, vinegar, and minced parsley. Shake them over the fire till quite hot, and serve immediately.

Tomato Joy.—*Ingredients:* 2 gallons of green tomatoes, 12 good sized onions, 2 quarts vinegar, 1 quart sugar, 2 tablespoonfuls salt, 2 tablespoonfuls mustard, same of pepper, (black), 1 tablespoonful allspice, same of cloves. *Mode:* Slice the tomatoes and onions, and stew in weak brine till tender, then strain. Put into a preserving pan 2 quarts vinegar, the sugar, salt, and spices, etc. When scalding hot add the tomatoes, and cook all slowly till you have a perfectly blended whole, stirring often, lest it burn. Put up in jars, cover tightly, and it will be fit to use in a week.

Sweet Pickled Pears.—Select firm, ripe fruit, and when peeled weigh, and for every 7 pounds of fruit allow 4 pounds of good white sugar, 1 pint of white vinegar, and ½ a tablespoonful each of whole cloves, whole allspice and cinnamon sticks.

Put the pears into a preserving pan and sprinkle the sugar over. Heat very slowly till the boiling point is reached, then add the vinegar and spices, and boil five or ten minutes (no more). Lift out the pears with a skimmer and spread them to cool. Boil the syrup till thick. Pack the pears in jars and pour the syrup boiling hot over them. Tie down, seal, and store for use.

Brandied Pears.—Select large, fine-flavoured pears, peel and cut in halves. To every pound of fruit allow a pound of sugar and about half a cup of good pale brandy. Make a syrup of the sugar and as much water as will dissolve it. Let it come to a boil, then put in the fruit and boil five minutes. Remove the pears and pack carefully into jars. Let the syrup boil fifteen minutes longer, or till it thickens well. Add the brandy, and remove the pan from the fire at once. Pour the hot syrup over the fruit, tie down and seal.

Pickles.—It is true that pickles can be purchased at every store or grocer's shop, just as jams of every kind can; but none, however well put up, are equal in flavour or actual goodness to home-made pickles and jams, made from the vegetables and fruits grown in one's own garden patch.

American housewives are very clever at both pickling and preserving, therefore I have secured a few of their best recipes from a lady correspondent residing in Virginia.

Cucumber Pickle.—Choose only cucumbers from two to

two and a half inches long, and be sure not one is specked or bruised. Pack them in a stone jar, strewing plenty of salt between each layer—using the coarsest salt. Cover the top gherkins completely with salt, and then pour in sufficient cold water to cover all, and close the jar. Leave them in this brine a full week, or ten days if it suits you. Then drain off the brine and look over the cucumbers again, and discard any that have become soft or bad, and lay the rest in fresh cold water for twenty-four hours longer, changing the water once during that time, after which proceed to the pickling proper.

Line a large enamel preserving pan with green grape vine leaves, and lay the cucumbers evenly upon them, and scatter about a teaspoonful of powdered alum over them, putting a little on each layer of cucumbers. The proportion of alum should be a teaspoonful to every two gallons of water.

Fill the preserving pan with cold water, having first covered the pickles three or four deep with more vine leaves. Put on it a close lid, and let it *steam* slowly for five or six hours, *not once* allowing it to come *to the boil*.

When the pickles are a fine green remove the leaves and throw the pickles into very cold water (iced if possible), and let them stand while you prepare the vinegar.

To every gallon of vinegar required allow 1 cup sugar, 3 dozen peppercorns, same of cloves, 1 dozen allspice, and a few blades of mace. Boil five minutes, pack the cucumbers into jars, and pour the vinegar scalding hot over them. Cover closely for two or three days, then strain off the vinegar, heat again and pour back. Repeat three times, at intervals of two, four, and six days ; then cover, tie down, and store in a dry place. In two months they will be ready to use.

Vegetable Stock.—*Ingredients :* 1 cabbage, 2 carrots, 1 turnip, 3 large onions, 1 tablespoonful butter, a bunch of herbs, 3 or 4 cloves, a few peppercorns, 3 quarts of water, salt to taste. *Mode :* Wash, scrape, and peel all the vegetables. Cut them up very small, and put into a stewpan with the butter, the herbs and seasoning. Let them fry gently or sweat in the butter for a few minutes, stirring constantly to prevent burning. Pour in three quarts of cold water, and salt to taste. When the water boils remove to the side of the fire and let it simmer gently for two hours or two and a half. Skim if necessary. Then strain the stock into a basin and put by for use.

Jelly from Chinese Gelatine.—*Ingredients :* 1 and a half sticks of Chinese gelatine, 4 cups cold water, 6 ounces sugar, 1 cup wine, or 2 tablespoonfuls of any strong spirit. (Rum makes a good flavouring.) ⅓ of an ounce of citric acid dissolved in a tablespoonful of boiling water. When spirit is used a few drops of cochineal will be required to colour the jelly. *Mode :* Break into small pieces the stick and a half of Chinese gelatine, and steep it for half an hour in four cups of cold water. Put it on to boil with the sugar, and boil till all is dissolved. Remove from the fire and add the wine or spirit according to taste, then the citric acid dissolved in boiling water. Pour into a mould and set away in a basin of cold water for three or four hours, when it will be ready to turn out.

Do not turn it out of the mould more than twenty minutes or so before it is required, or it will melt again.

Jelly, without Boiling.—*Ingredients :* 1 ounce Nelson's isinglass, 6 ounces sugar, ½ pint cold water, 1 pint boiling water, ½ pint sherry, ¼ or ⅓ of an ounce of citric acid dissolved in 1 tablespoonful boiling water. *Mode :* Soak the isinglass in ½ pint of cold water for ten minutes, add the sugar and stir well, then pour in the boiling water and stir till the isinglass is dissolved. Then add the wine, and lastly the citric acid dissolved in a little boiling water. Pour into moulds and set away in a cool place or on ice.

This jelly should be made over night in the hot weather.

Tomato Balls.—*Ingredients :* Some medium-sized tomatoes—the red, fleshy kinds are best—some ham, forcemeat, pastry, and bread crumbs. *Mode :* Cut the centres out of some tomatoes and restuff them with some good forcemeat made of ham, or ham paste, bread crumbs, herbs, butter, and an egg. Roll each stuffed tomato in a covering of thin pastry and drop them into boiling water for about fifteen minutes. Then take them out, roll in fine bread crumbs, and

fry in plenty of good fat till they are a golden brown.   Serve
with potato croquets.

Potato Souflés.—*Ingredients :* Four large potatoes
boiled in their skins, 1 tablespoonful butter, 3 eggs, salt,
pepper. *Mode :* The potatoes can be either boiled or baked ;
the latter is best.   When they are quite cooked, cut them in
halves, and scoop out as much of the potato as possible
without spoiling or breaking the skin. Put this into a
basin and mash it perfectly smooth, stir in the butter, pepper,
salt, yolks of the eggs, and the whites, well beaten. Now fill
the skins again, place them in an upright position in a baking
dish or cake tin, and bake quickly. Serve in a napkin.

Cocoa Cakes.—*Ingredients :* Two tablespoons butter, 2
tablespoons sugar, 1 cup flower, $\frac{1}{2}$ cup cocoa, 1 teaspoon
baking powder, 2 eggs, and a little milk. *Mode :* Mix the
butter, sugar, and eggs together. Mix the baking powder
with the flour and cocoa, and stir them in, adding a little
milk, if necessary, to thin the mixture, beat for a few minutes,
then pour into patty tins and bake in a quick oven. Time,
from fifteen to twenty minutes.

Dough Nuts.—*Ingredients :* Flour, baking powder, sugar,
butter, 2 eggs, and some jam or custard. *Mode :* Make a
paste of the flour, baking powder, sugar, butter, and eggs.
Roll out thin and cut into rounds, with a cutter or wine
glass.   Lay a spoonful of jam or thick custard on one round,
wet the edges, and lay another on top, pinch the two together
till the edges adhere, let them stand a few minutes, and then
fry in plenty of good lard or fat.

Lemon Cream.—*Ingredients :* Two tablespoons arrowroot, 2 cups boiling water, 1 small cup sugar, rind and
juice of 2 lemons, yolks and whites of 3 or 4 eggs. *Mode :*
Make the arrowroot with the boiling water, add the sugar,
first rubbed on the lemon rind, then the juice. Beat up the
whites of the eggs to a stiff froth. Mix the yolks with the
arrowroot mixture, and, lastly, stir in the whites, thickening
over a slow fire, pour into a mould, and when cold turn out
and serve with cream.

Cornflour Cakes.—*Ingredients :* $\frac{1}{4}$ pound packet of corn-flour, $\frac{1}{4}$ pound sugar, 1 tablespoonful butter, 1 teaspoonful baking powder, 2 eggs, 2 tablespoonfuls flour.   *Mode :* Mix the cornflour and flour together, rub in the butter, baking powder, and sugar.   Mix with the eggs well beaten, using a little milk if necessary.   Drop from a spoon on to the baking tin and bake in a hot oven.   Time about ten minutes.

Sultana Pudding.—*Ingredients :* 2 cups bread crumbs, $\frac{1}{2}$ cup flour, 2 tablespoonfuls dripping, 2 tablespoonfuls sugar, 1 cup sultanas, 1 teaspoonful mixed spice, a little candied peel, 1 teaspoonful baking powder, 2 or 3 eggs, some hot milk.   *Mode :* Pour about a cup of boiling milk over the bread, and when soaked beat in the flour by degrees, the dripping, sugar, spice, sultanas, candied peel, baking powder, lastly the eggs.   Pour into a basin or covered mould and either steam or boil from an hour to an hour and a half.

Gingerbread Pudding.—*Ingredients :* 1 cup flour, 2 cups bread crumbs, 2 teaspoonfuls ground ginger, 1 teaspoon-ful mixed spice, 1 teaspoonful baking powder, 2 tablespoon-fuls sugar, 1 cup golden syrup, 3 eggs, a little milk, 2 tablespoonfuls dripping.   *Mode :* Mix all the dry ingredients together, rub in the dripping.   Make a hole in the centre and pour in the golden syrup and the eggs, well beaten.   Mix all together, adding milk to thin it to a batter.   Pour into a buttered basin or mould and steam two hours.

Victoria Pudding.—*Ingredients :* 3 tablespoonfuls flour, 2 tablespoonfuls sugar, 1 tablespoonful butter, 1 egg-spoonful baking soda, 3 eggs, 3 or 4 teaspoonfuls jam, juice of 1 small lemon or lime, $\frac{1}{2}$ cup water.   *Mode :* Beat the sugar, butter, and eggs together.   Mix the soda with the flour and add it by degrees, beating till quite smooth, and thin with the water.   Stir in the jam, and lastly, just before pouring into the mould, the lemon juice.   Steam an hour and a half.

Bread and Fruit Pudding.—*Ingredients :* Some slices of fresh bread, 1 quart of gooseberries, or any small fruit, sugar to taste.   *Mode :* Line a basin or mould with pieces of bread,

not using the crust, and leave no vacant space. Stew some
fruit in water and sugar, and when cooked pour them into
the lined basin, put more bread on top, then a plate with a
weight on it, and leave the pudding till next day. Turn it
out and serve with boiled custard.

Pickles, Home-made.—Every large household should
make their own pickles; it is hardly worth while in a small
family where few vegetables are used. All hard vegetables
are suitable. Cabbage centres, cauliflowers, French beans,
young hard apples, radish pods, vegetable marrow, cucumbers,
eschalots. Make a very strong brine, and pour it boiling
over the vegetables to be pickled. When cold remove them
with a strainer and dry in the sun or oven, then pack into
bottles or jars. Pour over them the following:—Boil 1 gallon
white vinegar, with $\frac{1}{2}$ ounce each of black and white pepper,
mace, ginger, 2 peppercorns, 2 drams of cayenne pods or
bird's-eye chillies, 1 ounce cloves, and $\frac{1}{2}$ pound mustard. When
cold pour on to the pickles and cork tightly. If kept a few
months these will be equal to any imported pickles. All the
larger vegetables should be cut into pieces.

Pickles, Home-made.—*Ingredients:* Vegetables cut into
rounds, lengths and various shapes, 2 gallons vinegar, $1\frac{1}{2}$
allspice, chillies, 2 ounces ginger whole and tied in muslin,
2 teaspoonfuls cayenne, $1\frac{1}{2}$ pounds mustard. *Mode:* Having cut the vegetables into shapes, put them into a pan or
basin and sprinkle them with salt, leave them a couple of
days, then remove from the brine and dry in the sun. Boil
the vinegar with the spices and pour over the vegetables
when packed into jars or bottles.

Cauliflower and Cheese.—*Ingredients:* 1 cauliflower, 1
ounce butter, 1 ounce flour, 1 cup milk or water, a little
salt, pepper, and cayenne, 4 tablespoonfuls grated cheese.
Mode: Boil the cauliflower in a large saucepan of well-salted
water till tender, but not too soft. Then drain and lay it in
a dish with the flour uppermost. Melt the butter in a small
saucepan, mix in the flour smoothly, and add by degrees a
cup of milk, or water and milk, the pepper, cayenne, and half
the grated cheese. Stir well, and pour this sauce over the

cauliflower, then sprinkle the rest of the cheese over and set in a hot oven to brown. Serve with brown bread and butter.

Tomato Jam.—*Ingredients :* Tomatoes, lemons, loaf sugar. *Mode :* To every pound of peeled and sliced tomatoes allow 1 large lemon and 1 pound loaf sugar. Slice the lemons as for melon jam, and boil them with the tomatoes till tender before adding the sugar. Allow about ½ a cup of water to each pound of fruit.

Boil slowly and stir constantly, pour into jars when done, and when cold tie down. Time, about four hours to boil.

A Reliable Washing Fluid.—*Ingredients :* 5 pounds washing soda, 1½ pound fresh unslaked lime, 1 pound borax, 4 ounces ammonia (liquid). *Mode :* Pour 1 gallon of boiling water upon the soda and borax ; when it has thoroughly dissolved add the ammonia. Slake the lime in 1 gallon of hot water, and let it stand till quite settled, then pour the clear liquid off into the soda and borax water, and add 8 gallons more water. When soaking the clothes, add 1 cupful of this mixture to the water. It should be kept in a jar or bottles and corked down.

A Good Poultice.—Many a time the lonely Bushman suffers a martyrdom of pain from neuralgia, cold, earache, etc., etc., because he has nothing by him to alleviate it—or imagines he has nothing, yet while there are gum leaves to be got he can have nothing better. Let him cut the young leaves up very fine with his tobacco knife, mix them with some fat, if he has it, water if not, and boil them for a few minutes, then pour into a handkerchief or a clean woollen sock ; put this into the place where the pain is, and in a minute or two it will give relief.

Silver Soap.—*Ingredients :* ½ bar common soap, 1 table-spoonful whiting, 1 tablespoonful borax, 2 teaspoonfuls ammonia. *Mode :* Shred the soap very fine into an enamel saucepan, with sufficient water to prevent burning, when melted add a little more water, and stir in the whiting and the borax, remove from the fire and add the ammonia. Mix well, pour into a mould, and when cold turn out and place to harden. Rub on the silver with a flannel, then rinse and polish.

Tartar Sauce for Fish.—*Ingredients :* Yolk of 1 egg, ½ teaspoonful mustard, ½ small bottle of good olive oil, 2 tablespoonfuls white vinegar, or lemon juice if preferred, 1 tablespoonful onion juice, 1 tablespoonful chopped parsley, some capers. *Mode :* Put the yolk of 1 egg into a bowl, and stir it the one way with the bowl of a spoon, add the mustard, and when it is thoroughly blended drop the oil in very slowly, stirring all the time, and as it gets thick then with a few drops of vinegar or lemon juice. When the oil and vinegar are worked in add the onion juice and parsley, and about 3 tablespoonfuls of capers, chopped fine. Stir well together, add a dust of cayenne, and serve.

To Cook any Small Fish.—*Ingredients :* The fish, 1 egg, some very fine bread crumbs or biscuit dust, salt and pepper. *Mode :* When cleaned throw the fish into cold water and rinse them thoroughly ; then dry carefully on a coarse linen cloth, and dip each one separately into the beaten egg, and from that into the bread crumbs or biscuit dust, which has been well seasoned with pepper and salt. Lay them on a plate in a cool place for an hour, then fry in plenty of boiling oil or good fat till a delicate brown. Serve on a dish on which is laid a fringed napkin. Garnish with slices of lemon and send to table with tartar sauce.

Eggs and Cheese.—*Ingredients :* 3 or 4 eggs, grated cheese, tomato sauce, some buttered toast. *Mode :* Fry the eggs in some butter, turning up the edges to prevent the whites spreading too much. Lay them on buttered toast, and over each sprinkle some grated cheese and about a teaspoonful of tomato sauce. Put the dish into the oven for a few minutes, then serve. This makes a good breakfast dish.

Squab Pie.—*Ingredients :* 2 pounds chops, 2 pounds sour apples, sugar, allspice, salt, pepper, 1 onion, 1 cupful of gravy, some good pastry. *Mode :* Cut away most of the fat from the chops, and chop off the long bones. Peel, core, and slice the apples, and put a layer of them in the bottom of a pie dish, with a little sugar sprinkled over and some ground all-spice. Next put a layer of chops seasoned with pepper, salt, and some finely chopped onion. Continue this till the dish is full, pour in some gravy, and cover with pastry. Bake in a moderate oven for an hour and a half.

Salmon Jelly Moulds.—*Ingredients :* 1 tin salmon, 1 small packet gelatine, parsley, 1 small onion, 2 carrots, 6 or 8 peppercorns, 2 cloves, a little mace, salt, 1 tablespoonful chilli vinegar, 2 tablespoonfuls bread crumbs, 2 eggs. *Mode :* Soak the gelatine in a cup of cold water. Pour the liquor from a tin of salmon into a saucepan ; add the parsley, onion, and carrots, all cut up, the peppercorns, other spices, and half a cup of water, with the vinegar, a pinch of salt, and the gelatine, if soaked enough. Let this simmer till the vegetables are tender, then strain and pour over the salmon previously freed from all bones and skin. Stir in the bread crumbs and the hard-boiled eggs chopped up. Form this mixture into moulds by pressing into egg cups or wine glasses. Next morning turn out and serve with watercress or salad.

Savoury Rolls.—*Ingredients :* Some thin slices of cold beef, 1 tablespoonful of ham paste, bread crumbs, chopped parsley, thyme, grated lemon rind, pepper and salt, a little butter, some good stock or gravy, 1 egg, a little flour. *Mode :* Cut some thin slices of cold beef. Make a stuffing of the bread crumbs, herbs, ham paste, lemon rind and seasoning, moisten with 1 egg. Lay some of this stuffing on each slice of beef, roll it up and tie with tape or thread, flour them slightly and put into a stewpan with a little butter. Let them brown nicely, and then pour in some good stock or gravy. Simmer a few minutes and then serve with a dish of macaroni.

Luncheons.—Any woman can have a luncheon if money and time are of no importance. But it is the housewife who has to make £1 do the duty of £5 that deserves credit when she obtains a reputation for her dainty little dinners and luncheons.

As every experienced hostess knows, the table decorations and appointments are everything towards success. There

may only be very few dishes, but provided they are first-rate
and the table well dressed no one will notice that there are
not twenty or thirty.

Now that embroideries are so much used the arranging of
the table is greatly simplified.

The young hostess should be careful not to over-dress her
table, a fault even worse than the other extreme. She should
decide on her scheme of colour and work to it. For instance,
suppose she takes white and gold—of course the tablecloth
must always be of fine linen. In the centre of the table she
can have a pretty gold gilt basket of white and yellow
flowers, marguerites, with yellow centres, and a sprinkling
of maidenhair fern or asparagus foliage intermixed. The
handle of the basket can be wound round with broad ribbon
of the contrasting colours. Bread and butter plates should
be laid round, and beside each one two wine glasses. No
matter whether you have wine or not, the glassware dresses
the table. Lay three or four sets of knives and forks of
different sizes, according to the courses served.

Have several small glass dishes of various shapes and
sizes dispersed about the table. Two filled with pickles,
two more with candied fruits, two with olives, two with
sweets, then two larger with fruit salads, and two with
vegetable salads. These all give to the table a fine effect.
Let the napkins be prettily folded, and a single yellow rose
and its leaves placed on each, while in one of the wine glasses
(if you have no wine) place a tiny knot of flowers, which the
guests can make use of at once. If you have wine use long
specimen glasses, placed immediately in front of each place ;
decanters of wine, or lemon and raspberry syrup, can be placed
here and there, also glass water-bottles or jugs. If in the
summer have a couple of glass dishes filled with ice, if
you have no little ice brickets. Have the fruit prettily
arranged on the sideboard, or, if there is room on the table,
grouped artistically in the centre.

All the courses, which may be given according to the taste
and discretion of the hostess, should be exceptionally well
cooked and well served, the parlourmaid being neatly
dressed in a dark gown with white collar, cuffs, apron, and cap.

Nowadays a first course very often consists of cucumbers sliced, then oysters. Next game, an entree, a good salad. Then dessert, and lastly coffee, served in tiny cups, cheese and the fruit.

For the dessert there is great scope for the cook, as all sorts of cold puddings are allowable—blanc-manges, gelatine puddings, jellies, custards and creams.

Salt a Health Preserver.—If young people would only believe it, there is no greater health preserver than salt—common, ordinary table salt.

In the morning, immediately on getting up, take a vigorous scrubbing with hot water, soap, and a stiff flesh brush; then a douch with cold water well salted, and use a coarse bath towel to thoroughly dry the body.

Use salt with which to clean the teeth and to gargle the throat. Once a week take half a teaspoonful of salt dissolved in cold water. There is nothing to equal it as a health invigorator, to preserve the complexion, and keep one free from colds, fever, and, in fact, diseases of all sorts. You cannot have a better purifier.

Polishing Paste. — *Ingredients:* 1 pound soft soap, ½ pound rotten-stone, 1 quart rainwater. *Mode:* Mix the above ingredients together and boil them for half an hour, then pour into a jar, and when cold tie down. This paste will keep for years. For use apply it with a flannel or leather, polish with soft rags, and lastly with a leather dipped in whiting.

Lemon Sago.—*Ingredients:* 1 cup sago, 6 tablespoonfuls golden syrup, rind and juice of 2 lemons, a few drops essence of lemon. *Mode:* Boil the sago in 5 cups of water till quite clear, add the golden syrup, the lemon juice and the grated rind, and boil together a few moments, stir in the essence, and pour into a wet mould. When cold turn out and serve with boiled custard.

Potato Cheese Cake.—*Ingredients:* 3 or 4 boiled potatoes, 1 tablespoonful butter, 1 tablespoonful sugar, 2 eggs, grated peel and juice of 1 lemon, 2 teaspoonfuls brandy, and a few currants. *Mode:* Mash the 3 or 4 potatoes quite smooth. Melt the butter in a saucepan, and stir in the potato, the sugar, and eggs well beaten. Stir over the fire till it thickens, then add the grated peel and the lemon juice, the brandy, and lastly a few well-washed currants.

Fish Cake. — *Ingredients :* Some boiled fish, bread crumbs, 1 onion, 1 teaspoonful chopped parsley, 1 teaspoonful dripping, ½ cup milk, 2 eggs. *Mode :* Well grease a cake tin, and shake bread crumbs thickly round it, so as to form a coating. Mince the onion very fine and cook it in a small saucepan with the parsley and the dripping. Shred the fish free from all bones, and add it to the onion and parsley, and stir in 2 or 3 tablespoonfuls of bread crumbs, the milk, and the eggs, well beaten. Beat this mixture well, and pour into the cake tin, and bake nearly an hour. Turn out and serve with sauce.

Rabbit Croquettes.—*Ingredients :* One rabbit, an equal quantity of bacon or ham, some grated lemon-peel, chopped parsley, salt, cayenne, a little flour, and 1 or 2 eggs. *Mode :* Mince finely all the meat from a rabbit previously cooked, add to it the bacon or ham, also minced, season with the lemon-peel, and parsley, and cayenne to taste. Place all in a basin, add about a tablespoonful of flour and 1 egg. Mix well, and then form the meat into rolls, dip in egg, then in bread crumbs, and fry in boiling fat. Serve garnished with fried parsley.

Haricot Beans.—*Ingredients :* Beans, chopped parsley, butter, salt, pepper, a little lemon juice. *Mode :* Soak the beans for 12 hours, put them into a saucepan of cold water, and let them come to the boil gradually, then simmer till tender. Drain and put into a stewpan with some fresh butter, the chopped parsley, seasoning, and a little lemon juice squeezed over them, toss well together and serve very hot.

Macaronied Tomatoes.—*Ingredients :* 1 pound macaroni, 3 ounces butter, 3 ounces grated cheese, tomato sauce, pepper and salt. *Mode :* Have some boiling water well salted, and throw the macaroni into it. Let it boil till tender, but not pasty. Strain off all the water, and put into the saucepan the butter and cheese and tomato sauce. Keep tossing the macaroni till it gets well with the sauce, then serve very hot. *To make the sauce:* Take ripe tomatoes, wash, dry, and cut them up, put into a saucepan without any water, with salt, pepper, a few cloves, a little onion and celery, and boil till quite soft. Then pass through a sieve and pour into the macaroni.

Salad Dressing (to keep.)—*Ingredients:* Yolks of 2 eggs, 1 teaspoonful salt, 1 pint of the best salad oil, 1 tablespoonful of made mustard, 3 tablespoonfuls of vinegar, 1 of tarragon vinegar, 1 tablespoonful of lime juice, 1 teaspoonful pounded sugar, a dust of cayenne. *Mode:* Put the yolks of two raw eggs into a basin with the salt and mix well, then stir in, a few drops at a time, the oil; be sure to stir all the time, and when the oil is all mixed in add the mustard, then the vinegar, and lastly the sugar and lemon juice. Bottle and put away for use.

Cheese and Beans.— *Ingredients:* ½ pound haricot beans, 1 teaspoonful salt, chopped parsley, 2 or 3 small onions, 3 ounces grated cheese, 2 ounces butter, pepper. *Mode:* Soak the beans 24 hours, then rub off the skins, tie the beans in a cloth and boil in salted water for about 2 hours. Mince some parsley and the onions, and grate the cheese. When the beans are done drain them, turn them into a saucepan and mash them with a fork. Stir in the butter, parsley, and onion; season with salt and pepper, and beat the mixture till smooth. Pour into a well-greased pie-dish, put some pieces of butter on the top, and bake for one hour.

Apricot Pudding. — *Ingredients:* 1 tin of apricots, 2 slices of bread, some sugar, 2 ounces butter, 2 ounces sugar, 2 eggs, rind of ½ a lemon, 1 ounce grated bread crumbs or sponge cake. *Mode:* Place a couple of thin slices of bread, with the crusts cut off, in the bottom of a pie-dish. Pour the apricots and juice over this, and sprinkle some sugar on them; bake for 15 or 20 minutes. Put into a saucepan the butter, 2 ounces sugar, and dissolve over the fire; beat the eggs in a basin and pour the butter and sugar from the saucepan over them, add the grated lemon rind and bread crumbs or sponge cake. Beat this mixture well, and pour over the apricots. Bake in a moderate oven till a light brown.

Queen Cakes.—*Ingredients :* 1 pound flour, ½ pound currants, 1 teaspoonful baking-powder, a pinch of salt, grated rind of 1 lemon, ½ pound butter or dripping, 3 eggs, 1 teaspoonful lemon juice. *Mode :* Well wash the currants and dry in a cloth or the oven, put them into a basin with the flour, baking-powder, salt, and grated lemon rind. Beat the butter to a cream with the sugar, and eggs well beaten, stir into the dry ingredients, beat all together till well mixed, add the lemon juice, and fill small patty tins. Bake in a quick oven from 20 to 30 minutes.

American Dough-nuts.—*Ingredients :* 1½ pounds flour, 2 ounces butter, ½ pound sugar, 1 teaspoonful powdered cinnamon, a little nutmeg, 2 eggs, ½ cup yeast, and as much milk as will make a soft dough. *Mode :* Rub the butter into the flour, add the sugar and spices, then whisk the eggs, and add the yeast to them and the milk. Stir into the flour, and mix into a soft dough. Cover up, and leave to rise in a warm place. When sufficiently risen work into small balls, and throw into a saucepan of boiling lard ; be sure the fat is boiling, or the nuts will not be nice. Eat with or without jam.

Rhubarb Fritters.—*Ingredients :* Some young rhubarb, 6 tablespoonfuls flour, 1 pint milk, 2 or 3 eggs, a pinch of salt, some powdered sugar. *Mode :* Peel and cut some young rhubarb into lengths of 2 or 3 inches. Make a smooth batter with the eggs, flour, and milk, add a pinch of salt. Then dip each piece of rhubarb into it, and fry in boiling fat quickly till a good colour. Serve very hot, piled on a dish, and plenty of powdered sugar over them.

Baked Cod Fish.—*Ingredients :* 1 cod fish, some forcemeat, 1 egg, some bread crumbs. *Mode :* Having carefully cleaned the fish, stuff it with the ordinary forcemeat and sew up the opening. Brush the fish over with the beaten egg, and sprinkle thickly with bread crumbs. Lay in a greased or buttered baking tin, and bake in a hot oven. When the fish will easily separate from the bones it is ready to serve.

Dressing for Cold Cabbage.—*Ingredients:* 2 eggs, 1 tablespoonful butter or oil, 1 tablespoonful sugar, 1 cup vinegar, 1 tablespoonful mustard, a little pepper. *Mode:* Beat the eggs, butter, and sugar together, add the mustard (mixed) and the vinegar by degrees. Put into a small jug, and stand in a saucepan of boiling water to cook, stirring carefully to prevent it curdling. Cut the cabbage very fine, salt and pepper it, and pour the dressing over it. Serve for luncheon or supper.

Herb Essence.—*Ingredients:* 1 penny bunch each of thyme, sage, marjoram, 1 pint of good white vinegar, 1 tablespoonful salt, 1 teaspoonful pepper, or half that of cayenne, 1 tablespoonful of whisky. *Mode:* Put the herbs on to boil in about 1 pint of water, and boil very slowly to extract all the flavour. When reduced to half a pint add the vinegar and boil a few minutes longer, adding the salt and pepper. Remove from the fire, and when cold strain and bottle, adding the whisky last of all as a preservative. 1 tea or tablespoonful, according to size, will flavour a stew, hash, or mince.

Anchovy Eggs.—*Ingredients:* Some good puff paste, 6 eggs, 1 tablespoonful anchovy paste, 1 teaspoonful onion juice, 1 teaspoonful chopped parsley, 1 teaspoonful butter, cayenne. *Mode:* Boil the eggs hard, peel them and cut them in half, scoop out the yolks into a basin with the anchovy paste, parsley, butter, and onion juice; season to taste, and when these are all smoothly mashed into a stiff paste, fill the eggs, put the halves together, and enclose each egg in puff paste. Bake in the oven, or fry in boiling fat. Serve very hot, or they can be eaten cold for supper.

Fricassied Eggs.—*Ingredients:* 3 or 4 eggs, 1 teaspoonful chopped onion, 1 teaspoonful parsley, pepper, salt, 1 teaspoonful anchovy sauce, a little milk, 1 teaspoonful cornflour. *Mode:* Boil the eggs hard. When done, put them into cold water for a few minutes, then peel the shells off, cut them in half, and from the rounded end cut a little slice, so that they will stand upright. Scoop out the yolks, put them into a basin with the onion, parsley, and seasoning. Mash these ingredients together, and fill the eggs. Lay them carefully in boiling fat, and fry a light brown. Make a sauce with some milk and anchovy paste or sauce, a dust of cayenne, thicken it with a little cornflour, and having arranged the eggs neatly on the dish, pour the sauce, very hot, round them.

Savoury Balls.—*Ingredients:* 5 ounces flour, 2 ounces suet, 1 teaspoonful parsley (chopped), 2 sprigs of dried thyme, 1 small teaspoonful baking-powder, teaspoonful chopped onion, pepper, salt, stock or water to make a stiff paste. *Mode:* Put the suet through the mincing machine till quite smooth, then rub it into the flour and other dry ingredients. Mix into a paste with the stock, and mould into balls. Grease a small steamer, and steam about 1 hour. Serve with soup or stew.

Salmon Savoury.—*Ingredients:* 1 tin of salmon, 1 ounce gelatine, 1 cup cold water, 1 onion, 1 carrot, a few peppercorns, cloves, 1 blade of mace, 1 tablespoonful chilli vinegar, salt, 2 tablespoonfuls bread crumbs, a little parsley. *Mode:* Soak the gelatine in about 1 cup of water. Pour the liquid from a tin of salmon into a saucepan, add to it the parsley (chopped fine), the onion and carrot (sliced), then the spices, salt, and vinegar, mixed with half a cup of cold water. When the gelatine is soft turn it in too, and let it all boil gently till the vegetables are tender. It may require a little more water if there is not much liquid with the salmon. When the vegetables are tender, strain through a sieve over the salmon, which must have been freed from all skin and bone, and to which has been added the bread crumbs and the hard-boiled egg finely minced. Stir all together, and pour into a wet mould or basin; garnish with parsley or hard-boiled egg. This makes a very pretty luncheon or supper dish.

Killing Day on a Station.—This is the most anxious time for the housekeeper on a cattle station, on account of the amount of meat she has to find ways and means of utilising and preserving, so that she shall be able to have soup and fresh meat as long as possible. In the summer it is nearly impossible to have fresh meat for more than a week after killing day. Where the killing is weekly this is right enough, but on many stations, where only a few "hands" are kept, killing day only comes when the beef has all run out, and that may be but every three weeks or every month.

In old times it was not unusual, on some far out stations, to kill only every three months. Then it was the lady housewife had a chance to show her skill and inventive ingenuity, and, difficult as it often was to provide appetising dishes, I must say there was very great pleasure and some excitement in it. Killing is usually done in the afternoon, towards 4 or 5 o'clock, and invariably that evening's meal consists of liver and bacon, with usually the sweetbread also fried. In cooking the liver when so fresh it is apt to become hard and brown before it is done. To avoid this, when it is cut into pieces place them in a deep dish and pour some hot— not boiling—water over. Let them lie in this a few minutes, and remove to the pan without drying. It will then fry soft.

The brains make a nice breakfast dish for next morning. But they must be well washed, freed from all blood, and left all night in salt and water. Next morning wash again, and throw into a saucepan of fast boiling water for about two minutes. Then remove to the board, cut into convenient pieces, dip in egg, roll in bread crumbs, and fry in boiling fat. There is always steak for breakfast as well, and being so fresh it is usually rather tough. If there are paw-paws growing on the place, and the fruit is any size at all, slice one up into a little warm water, and soak the steak in this twenty or thirty minutes. The riper the fruit the better for the purpose, but I have had good results from the unripe used as I say. Wash and dry the meat after it has been soaked, then fry. Failing the paw-paws, beat it well, and chop lightly with a butcher's knife, before grilling or frying. The soup is the most important matter, as the housewife, of course, wants to have soup as long as possible. The only way to have it right through, from killing to killing, is by making a very strong extract, and to do this the bones must be smashed as small as possible. There should be a special pot for the soup making, large enough to hold the amount required. When the bones have been broken and smashed small as possible, fill the pot up with water, and let it boil *slowly* for the first two or three hours. The housewife will find it a very great convenience to have a tap to the soup pot. When living on the station I had a large oblong tin boiler made by a tinsmith, and a tap inserted in it, so that I was able every day to draw off sufficient stock for the dinner from the bottom and free from all fat. Such a pot as I mean will only cost a few shillings, and the comfort and utility of it will be found inestimable. It is advisable to have beef-tea for the first day, as the stock will not be ready. At the end of the first day, or when it has been on ten or twelve hours, some of the bones may be removed and other fresh ones put in, and the pot filled up. Keep the pot boiling slowly, day and night if possible. Sufficient stock for next day can be drawn off each night, and it should be in a stiff jelly by the morning, when every particle of fat can be taken off in a cake. Managed in this way there should be stock for a fortnight, for when it is in a stiff jelly one cup of it to two of water will be quite strong enough to use. When the meat and bones are exhausted, a fowl can be added; no matter how old, it will make soup; the heads, legs, giblets of chickens, that have been killed for the table, the hindquarters of a wallaby, a kangaroo tail, and any wild fowl or small birds, so long as they are properly cleaned and chopped up, will make stock. And when there is nothing else, pease soup can always be made. Let me impress the fact that *no particle* of vegetable must be introduced into the stock pot; the *least little* bit of onion or carrot will make it ferment once it gets cold; for which reason, when scraps of cooked poultry are thrown into the stock pot, any stuffing that may be adhering to them must be scraped off. Salt is the only thing that should be added to the meat.

A strong concentrated essence of beef can be made by boiling down bones and meat, but that is hardly necessary unless killing days are very far apart. Many of the choicest portions of the beast are not used at all on the station, simply because they will not keep till the other parts have been utilised. The cheek, for instance, is seldom or never used, yet it is quite possible to pickle this portion, and it becomes a pleasant change later on. The chief reason it is not used

is on account of the cleaning. If the housewife gets one of
the men to cut the cheeks off roughly for her, she can skin
them herself in a few minutes. I would advise the housewife, who is a good cook, or who takes a pride in her table,
to have a small private harness cask, where she can pickle
many unconsidered tit-bits as a stand-by. The feet, too, are
generally left for the fat-pot, or thrown away altogether.
Yet they are not troublesome to clean, and make a delicious
dish. To clean them, soak a few minutes in very hot water,
dip quickly into cold, and scrape the hair off. If it will not
come readily, dip them a second or third time into the hot
water. When quite clean, they too can be kept in pickle till
needed.

Recipes will be found farther on for ox-cheek and cow-heel.
There are also recipes for pickles suitable for the purpose I
have mentioned.

Another thing that should be made each killing time is
what is usually called German sausage. I often found them
a great stand-by for breakfast, particularly on mornings
when the gentlemen wanted an early start, or when they
came in hungry from the yards after drafting or branding.

German Sausage.—*Ingredients :* 3 pounds beef, 2 pounds
bacon, salt, saltpetre, pepper, 1 tablespoonful spice. *Mode :*
Choose a piece of lean beef and salt it well, using a little
saltpetre to colour it. When the beef is sufficiently salted,
which should be in two or three days, cut it up, and with the
bacon pass through the mincing machine, add pepper and
spice, and fill a well-cleaned skin, tie securely at both ends,
and boil for a couple of hours. When cold hang in the chimney to smoke.

To Cook Cow-Heel.—*Ingredients :* Two cow-heels, a
bunch of herbs, 1 carrot, 1 turnip, 1 onion, bread crumbs,
dripping or butter. *Mode :* Having thoroughly cleaned the
cow-heels, put them on to boil with the vegetables for about
three hours, letting them do very slowly. When soft remove
on to the board, and take out the bones. Now take a deep
dish, lay the cow-heel upon it, with a little salt and pepper,
cover with a layer of bread crumbs, put some little bits of

butter over, pour about a cup of the soup round, and bake in a brisk oven till brown. This makes a nice luncheon dish cold.

German Sausage.—*Ingredients :* 3 pounds of pickled beef, 2 cow-heels, 2 pounds of bacon, 1 pound of suet, salt, pepper, sage. *Mode :* Boil the cow-heels, and remove the bones, boil the beef and bacon slightly, cut all up into small pieces, with the suet, and pass the whole through the mincing machine. Parch the sage in the oven, and rub in the hand to powder, add pepper and a little salt, and about half a teaspoonful of powdered saltpetre. Take a well-washed skin, run it on to the nozzle of the mincing machine, and put the meat through again, filling the skin evenly and firmly.

When full tie securely at both ends, prick here and there to prevent bursting, and put down to boil slowly for an hour or two. When cold hang in the chimney to be smoked. Two or three of these should be made every killing on a station, as they make an excellent stand-by for breakfast or luncheon, when the meat has run out.

Oyster Cream (a Soup).—*Ingredients :* 2 quarts of oysters, 1 quart sweet milk, 2 blades mace, 2 tablespoonfuls butter, 3 tablespoonfuls flour, salt, pepper. *Mode :* Put the oysters with their liquor into a stewpan over a slow fire ; when the scum rises skim off every particle. Let the oysters boil one minute, and then press them through a sieve, using the bowl of a silver spoon, and keeping them moist with the liquor, so that they will go through. In another stewpan put the milk and mace, stand by the fire where it will heat gradually ; blend the flour and butter together smoothly with a little cold milk, and stir it into the hot milk. Next stir in the oyster pulp very gradually, season with pepper and salt, and serve in a tureen with the following croûtons :—

To make the croûtons make a thick batter with 1 egg, flour, and a little milk. Pour this into a flannel bag, and squeeze it drop by drop into a pan of boiling fat. When they are a light brown drain on kitchen paper, place in the bottom of the tureen, and pour the soup over them.

Marrow Toast.—Take the marrow-bone out of a round of beef—this is a dish that might be enjoyed every killing time on a station, as the best marrow-bones are generally thrown into the fat pot—saw the bones into lengths of one or two inches as far as the marrow extends. Place each piece in the centre of a small thin slice or square of bread, and place these in the bottom of a dripping pan; sprinkle the marrow with a little salt. Then put the pan into a hot oven, and do not remove till the bread is browned. Surround each ring of bone with a fringe of white paper, and serve on small plates.

Chicken in Curry Mask.—*Ingredients :* 1 chicken, 1 cup bread crumbs, half cup of flour, 1 tablespoonful cream, 2 or 3 eggs, 1 heaped teaspoonful curry paste or powder, salt, milk to thin it to a batter. *Mode :* The chicken can be either boiled or baked. Carve into neat joints; make a batter with the bread crumbs, flour, eggs, cream, curry powder and milk dip each piece of chicken in and coat it well with this mixture, then fry in plenty of boiling fat. Arrange on a dish, and garnish with hard-boiled egg. Can be eaten hot or cold.

Green Tomato Chutney.—*Ingredients :* 1 peck green tomatoes, 12 small pickling onions, 12 green chillies, salt, $\frac{1}{2}$ pound mustard seed, 1 tablespoonful each of ground cloves, cinnamon, allspice, and mace, 1 gallon vinegar, 2 pounds brown sugar. *Mode :* Slice the tomatoes, onions, and chillies, and place in a large jar or basin with a few spoonfuls of salt over it. Let it stand twelve hours, then turn into an enamel preserving pan, and add the spices, the vinegar, and sugar and let the pickle boil till tender. It must do very slowly Pour into jars, and when cold tie down. If properly made will keep any time.

For Afternoon Tea.—For a fashionable afternoon tea the table should be set in the rear of the drawing-room, or, if there are two rooms, in the smaller of them. Coloured cloths are usually used, and the table can be decorated with baskets of flowers and fruit. Do not set the plates, etc., round, but let them be placed in piles of threes and fours here and there, with knives, forks, and spoons where they can be quickly found when required. A few table-napkins beside them (the smaller the napkins the better). The tea equipage should be on a separate table.

Russian tea is generally preferred at this time. All sorts of candied fruits and delicate tit-bits are served.

For Afternoon Tea.—Serve rolled bread and butter, sandwiches made of ham paste, potted ham, tongue, or chicken. The crusts of the bread should be cut off, and the sandwiches cut into three-corner shapes or fingers. Anchovy sandwiches, or those made with cheese paste, are liked by gentlemen.

Salads are allowable nowadays at afternoon teas; egg, oyster, or chicken, are suitable served with brown bread and biscuits.

Cakes for this purpose should be very small.

Wine and cordial should always be on the sideboard; claret cup or champagne cup on the table.

Cheese Paste.—*Ingredients :* 1 pound cheese, 1 tablespoonful mustard, cayenne, 1 tablespoonful butter. *Mode :* Grate the cheese, then pound it in a mortar with the dry mustard, cayenne, and butter. Press into small pots, and tie down for use. Excellent for sandwiches.

Russian Tea.—Into each cup put one or two lumps of sugar, a thin slice of lemon, and 1 teaspoonful old rum. Pour the tea over. Ceylon tea is generally used. The rum can be omitted where not liked, but it greatly improves the flavour.

Sheep's Liver.—*Ingredients :* 1 sheep's liver, 2 onions, 1 apple, 1 cupful bread crumbs, sage, flour, seasoning, dripping. *Mode :* Wash the liver in cold water, and dry it well. Prepare the stuffing as follows : chop up the onion and apple very small, powder a teaspoonful of sage, add the bread crumbs, and season to taste. Sew up the sides and one end of the liver, place the stuffing in the centre, and then sew that up too. Place in the baking-pan with some lard or dripping and a cupful of water. Bake in a moderate oven for an hour, and baste well. When cooked draw out the threads.

For the gravy skim the fat off the liquor in the pan, blend 2 teaspoonfuls of flour with water, and stir it over the fire till it thickens. Serve over the liver.

Hot Pot.—*Ingredients :* ½ pound good steak or stewing

beef, $\frac{1}{2}$ pound mutton off the neck, 1 onion, 6 potatoes, seasoning. *Mode:* Pound the steak with the rolling-pin, and
cut both it and the mutton into pieces about an inch square,
or smaller if preferred, peel and slice the onion and potatoes.
Take a pie-dish, and first put a layer of potatoes, then a layer
of meat, sprinkle the onion over and any dried herbs liked,
pepper and salt. Repeat this till the dish is filled, and finish
with a thick layer of potatoes. Now take about a pint of
stock or water, salt it slightly, and, if liked, add a tablespoonful of vinegar to it. Pour this over the contents of the
dish, cover with a plate, and bake in a rather brisk oven;
ten or fifteen minutes before serving remove the plate, and
allow the potatoes to brown. Serve in the dish. Time to
bake, an hour and a half.

Haricot Mutton.—*Ingredients :* 2 pounds neck of mutton,
1 carrot, 1 turnip, 1 onion, seasoning, a little flour, 1 teaspoonful sauce. *Mode :* Divide the neck into chops, and cut
each in two, then fry them a few minutes just to brown the
outside. Scrape the carrot, and cut into slips lengthwise, peel
and slice the turnip and onion, and having removed the chops
from the pan, put the vegetables into the fat, and fry them
slightly. Put all into a stewpan with salt, pepper, and about
a cup and a half of water ; cover, and simmer slowly. When
done blend a spoonful of flour with water, and a little sauce,
and stir it into the gravy. Time, one hour and a half.

Foam Balls for Soup.—*Ingredients :* For a large tureen
of soup, 1 cup bread crumbs, 1 heaped spoonful dripping,
pepper, salt, 1 or 2 eggs, flour to mould the balls. *Mode :*
Mix the bread crumbs and dripping together, add the seasoning, and break the eggs in without beating ; mix well with
a fork. Then flour the hands and mould into little balls.
Let them stand about half an hour to harden, then throw into
the boiling soup about twenty minutes before serving.

Nut-balls for Soup.—*Ingredients :* Some boiled rice, nuts,
1 or 2 eggs, salt, bread crumbs. *Mode :* Any nuts preferred
can be used, but the small, round Barcelona are the best.
Shell as many as are required, being careful not to smash or
bruise them ; mould the rice round each nut (only practice

will make perfect), dip into beaten egg, and roll in fine
bread crumbs. Fry these balls in boiling fat till a light
brown, and five minutes before serving throw them into the
soup, or they can be placed in the tureen and the soup poured
over them.

Anchovy-balls for Fish-soup.—*Ingredients:* 1 cup
bread crumbs, 1 tablespoonful anchovy paste, 1 egg, 2 teaspoonfuls dripping, pepper, parsley. *Mode:* Mix the bread
crumbs, dripping, and anchovy paste together, and 1 teaspoonful of finely-chopped parsley, break the egg into the
mixture, or if too dry use two eggs, but do not have it too
moist, or the balls will break in the boiling. Mould into
marbles, fry in boiling fat, and pour the soup over them in the
tureen.

About Salads.—There is nothing that looks cooler on the
table than a dish of freshly-made green salad, and there is
hardly any dish so wholesome or so cheap, yet in how few
houses is it considered an article of regular diet, and how
very seldom is it nicely dressed! I intend, therefore, pre-
paratory to giving recipes for salads to give a few useful
hints and directions as to the choice of materials where it is
not always possible to get what we consider proper or in
general use.

Salads, as a rule, are made of lettuce, beetroot, endive,
celery, tomato, radish, onions, cucumber, etc. From these
various combinations are made, and they can be variously
dressed with lobster, crab, salmon, chicken, tongue, fish and
vegetables. Then there are sweet or fruit salads, equally
cool and delicious, made with dressings of wines, jellies,
custards, or syrups.

The salad is one of those small household matters which
should be undertaken by the mistress or one of the daughters
of the house, because, as a rule, the cook is too busy and
too hurried to give the attention and time necessary for the
production of a perfect salad, and anything less is not appetising, or as it should be : the dressing may be lumpy or greasy,
the lettuce wilted. How many people refuse salad dressing
because of the salad oil which flavours it. This is not right;

the oil should not be perceptible, though there it should be, so incorporated that there is no oily flavour at all. And it is just in the mixture of the oil with the yolks of the eggs that such patience is required, as if mixed in too quickly, or more than a few drops at a time, the oil curdles and becomes unpalatable. I will now give detailed directions for a lobster salad, and readers can bear in mind that all are made similar, the only difference being in the materials used, and from which the salad always takes its name.

Children's Meals.—Children should have their meals as regularly as possible, and if they require anything between, it should be as little and as light as possible, something more to stay the appetite rather than to satisfy it.

It is very often a mistake to forbid the little ones to have anything between their meals, as there are many children who can only eat just at the moment they feel hungry, and if kept waiting are apt to get sick and faint, and lose all desire for food later on. Even if a child asks for something to eat in the middle of the night, I think it should be given. A parent or nurse can generally tell whether the craving is genuine or not, and while satisfying and humouring the little one she should endeavour to so manage that it shall not happen as a regular thing.

Impatience and ill-temper will never do any good; entire and complete sympathy will win any and every little one, and will very soon break down and do away with irritability and fractiousness. Children have their bad times, their aches, pains, and hours of nervous depression and imaginings, just as we children of an older growth have, and just as sympathy and tenderness soothes and cheers us, so it will them. Thus, when a child wakes in the night and says she is hungry, the mother or nurse will do better to offer sympathy and a few tender words as she rises to comply with the request for bread and butter, than to lose her temper, and tell the child to go to sleep or be smacked. Probably a mouthful or two and the child will drop to sleep again satisfied, whereas without just that little morsel of food she may be awake restless and nervous for hours. Mothers often declare that such cravings are "only fancy." So they are undoubtedly, but such fancies are as real to the child as the sternest reality.

In many houses it is a hard and fast rule that there shall be no eating between meals, and children who need it are considered pampered and spoilt. Believe me, you of my readers who are mothers, many little ones actually require something between meals, and should have it for health's sake, if it be but a biscuit or crust of bread and drink of milk.

Just as great pains should be taken in the preparation of children's food as in that for adults. Simple as the food may be it, nevertheless, requires careful preparation. Late dinners and richly seasoned food towards bedtime are very bad for children; they should have their dinner in the middle of the day, and if this is impossible, on account of their school hours, let them take a light luncheon to school with them, and have a good dinner ready for them when they get home. About the best arrangement for children attending school is to give them a generous and wholesome breakfast at eight o'clock of oatmeal porridge, scones, or bread and butter or jam, with a cup of coffee or milk; a light luncheon of sandwiches, made of egg, ham paste, or something of the kind, and fruit of one kind or another. My children are very fond of egg pasties, made as follows: Cover a good-sized patty tin with paste, break an egg into it, dust salt and pepper over it, cover with paste, and bake. Fruit pasties can be made in the same way, and they always carry well. At three, or half-past three o'clock, when they return from school, let them have a good dinner of meat, vegetables, and a light pudding; and at seven o'clock their tea or supper of bread and jam or butter, watercress, or for very young children bread and milk or cornflour, Honey is excellent for the little ones, and golden syrup is a pleasant change. For the morning meal boiled rice, germia, or bread and milk can take the place of porridge when preferred. I would warn mothers that oatmeal does not always agree with children, indeed there are some constitutions it decidedly disagrees with. Stewed fruit, poached eggs, omelets, all are excellent for the morning meal, with cocoa, chocolate, coffee, or milk for beverages.

For dinner, the best meats for children are beef and mutton,

D

fowl and fish, soup and broth, all are good. Vegetables of all kinds, provided they are well cooked ; tomatoes are especially wholesome, and can be stewed with apples if liked. For puddings, light puddings made with milk, blanc-mange, and boiled batter.

It is a great mistake to force a child to eat what he or she does not like. Let them have what they prefer, and leave what they do not like. If possible, it is best to make them eat what they take on to their plates, but I would never enforce it. A child may be helped too largely, or may suddenly feel unable to finish what he has. " Put yourself in his place," is the maxim I would follow always. The fashion of making children eat fat, on the score that it is good for them, and certain vegetables that they dislike, is, in my opinion, simply barbarous.

Stewed Beefsteak.—*Ingredients:* The under-cut of a sirloin of beef, 1 ounce butter, a little flour, 2 carrots, 2 or 3 eschallots, salt, pepper, toasted bread. *Mode:* Cut the meat into thick slices, score them across and dredge flour over them. Lay them in a stewpan with the butter, let the butter absorb into the meat, but do not let it brown. Now slice the carrots and eschallots, and add them with the salt and pepper. Cover with water, and stew gently for two hours. Serve on toasted bread, with the carrots and gravy round.

Swiss Toast.—*Ingredients:* Some thin slices of toast, milk, 1 egg, cinnamon, and powdered sugar. *Mode:* Dip the slices of toast into milk, brush over with egg, and sift sugar and powdered cinnamon on them. Fry quickly in boiling fat till a golden brown. Serve with boiled arrowroot or corn-flower.

Hotch-potch.—*Ingredients:* 3 onions, 3 carrots, herbs, 1 cabbage, ½ pint of peas, 1 cauliflower, 2 turnips, 1 teaspoonful sugar, salt, 8 peppercorns, 3 or 4 potatoes, 5 pints water, 2 pints milk. *Mode:* Prepare all the vegetables and put them on to boil in 5 pints of water. Let it boil slowly for four hours. Then strain through the colander, and pulp the vegetables through a sieve. Return them to the stock, and add the seasoning and the milk. Let it simmer gently by the side of the fire till required. Pour into the tureen over a few slices of toast and serve.

French Beans on Toast.—*Ingredients:* Some boiled French beans, butter, 1 lemon and a little parsley, toast. *Mode:* Cut or shred the beans delicately, and boil in salted water with a pinch of soda. Strain through a colander, and when all the water is pressed out throw them into a frying-pan, with sufficient boiling butter to cook them without browning. Fry a few minutes. Have some buttered toast arranged on a dish, heap the beans on to it, sprinkle a little parsley over, and serve with slices of lemon to garnish.

Asparagus Salad.—*Ingredients:* Some cold, boiled aspa-ragus, cucumber, mayonnaise sauce, some cold tongue or prawns. *Mode:* Arrange the asparagus with the sliced cucumber, cover with a rich mayonnaise sauce, and decorate with prawns or cold tongue, cut into fanciful shapes.

To Boil Cabbage.—Choose well-grown, but not old cabbage. Cut into quarters, and remove all the coarse out-side leaves. Let it steep for half an hour in salt and water, to clear it from grubs and sand. Have a saucepan of boiling water in which is a good teaspoonful of coarse salt, a small nut of soda, and half a teaspoonful of sugar. Plunge the cabbage in, and let it boil fast with the *lid of the saucepan off*. When leaves and stalk are tender strain, and be sure and press out all water. Put into the vegetable dish, and cut across to let the steam out.

Cabbage Pie.—*Ingredients:* Any cold cabbage left from dinner, potatoes, a little butter, seasoning, and bread crumbs, 2 eggs. *Mode:* Mash the cabbage and potato together thoroughly, season with pepper and salt, and stir in a little butter. Put into a pie-dish, and cover with a layer of bread crumbs, beat up the eggs and moisten the bread crumbs all over evenly, then bake in a quick oven till slightly browned. Time, about twenty minutes to brown.

Vegetable Marrow Cutlets.—*Ingredients:* 1 vegetable marrow, 2 onions, a bunch of herbs, seasoning, a little stock or milk, bread crumbs, 2 eggs. *Mode:* Peel and remove the seeds from a large vegetable marrow. Cut into pieces and shape into cutlets. Lay them in a stewpan with the onions sliced, the herbs, and enough stock or milk to just cover them. Stew till they are nearly done, *not soft*, drain and dry them in a cloth. Brush them over with egg, and then sift plenty of seasoned bread crumbs over them. Let them stand for an hour, then arrange in a frying basket, and fry in boiling fat a light brown.

Potato Corks.—*Ingredients :* 1 pound of mashed potato, 1 ounce butter, 5 eggs, salt, nutmeg, ½ teaspoonful sugar, 2 tablespoonfuls cream, flour to roll in. *Mode :* Rub the potato through a sieve into a basin, stir in the butter, the seasoning, the yolks of the 5 eggs, and lastly the cream. Turn this mixture out on to the floured board and roll it into cork-shaped pieces about three inches long and half as thick. Let them stand for a little while, then fry in butter or good dripping, browning them on all sides.

Curried Cauliflower.—*Ingredients :* 2 small or 1 large cauliflower, 1 onion, 3 ounces butter, 1 apple, 1 potato (boiled), 1 tablespoonful cocoanut, ½ pint stock, 1 teaspoonful curry powder, salt, pepper, and a pinch of sugar, 1 tablespoonful cream, 1 teaspoonful browned flour, 1 tablespoonful lemon juice or vinegar. *Mode :* Boil the cauliflower in salted water till tender. Slice the onion, the apple, and potato, and fry in part of the butter. Add the cocoanut when the onion, etc., is brown. Pour in the stock, blend the curry powder, and add it with the salt, pepper, and pinch of sugar. Boil a few minutes, then strain away the vegetables, and return the sauce to the saucepan with the cream or milk, the rest of the butter, and thicken with the browned flour and a little more curry powder. Cook three or four minutes. Divide the cauliflower into sprigs, and drop them into this sauce about five minutes before serving. Sprinkle the lemon juice over, or garnish with slices of lemon.

Another way is to place the whole cauliflower in an *entrée* dish and pour the boiling curry sauce over it. Serve with boiled rice round the edge of the dish, or in a separate dish.

Pigweed and Cheese.—Use only the young and tender shoots ; wash them well and tie in bunches. Throw into fast boiling salt and water in which is a little bit of soda. Boil till tender, then drain and chop small, grate some cheese. Arrange a layer of pigweed on a dish, and sprinkle about a tablespoonful of vinegar over it, then a layer of cheese, another layer of pigweed, some little bits of buttr,e and some made mustard, then the rest of the cheese and some more butter. Bake in a hot oven about half an hour.

Pigweed to Boil.—Choose only those shoots that have not flowered, tie in bunches, and wash thoroughly. Have some water, salted and with a bit of soda in it, boiling. Throw in the pigweed and boil fast till tender. Serve with melted butter over it.

Pigweed Salad.—Pick only the young and tender shoots, tie in small bunches, wash thoroughly, and throw into fast boiling water, in which is a tiny pinch of soda and a teaspoonful of salt. Boil till tender, then drain, and serve with a good salad dressing over, and garnish with hard-boiled or pickled eggs.

Almond Cheesecake.—*Ingredients:* Equal weight of eggs and butter, two-thirds their weight of sugar, half weight of pounded almonds, the grated rind of 1 or 2 lemons. *Mode:* Beat the eggs, butter, and sugar together in an enamel saucepan, put on to the fire, and when melted stir in the pounded almonds and grated lemon-peel. Stir over the fire for half an hour, or till the mixture is the consistency of cream or treacle. Pour into small pots, and when cold cover with brandy paper and tie down.

Melon and Pineapple Jam.—*Ingredients:* 1 pie or snow melon. To every 4 pounds allow 1 pineapple and 1 large lemon, and ¾ pound sugar to the pound of fruit, 2 ounces of ginger, bruised. *Mode:* Cut up the melon, pineapples, and lemons overnight, and put half the sugar to it. Next morning put it on to boil slowly, and when the lemon-peel is soft put in the rest of the sugar. Boil till it is clear.

Melon Jam.—Cut the pie melon up overnight into pieces about an inch square. To 12 pounds of melon allow about 6 lemons, slice them thin, cutting rind and pulp together. If

so much lemon-peel is not liked reduce it, but the juice of
6 lemons will not be too much for 12 pounds of melon.
Allow 9 pounds of sugar, or ¾ pound to the pound. Put about
half of it on the fruit overnight to make syrup. Put it on to
boil in the morning, and when the lemon-peel is tender put
in the rest of the sugar. Boil slowly till it becomes clear.
Ginger can be added if liked.

Food Value of the Bush.—In the far Bush the housewife is very often at her wits end to know what to do for
a change of diet. If a time of drought, or should there be
no vegetable garden attached to the station, she has generally
to fall back upon preserved and tinned vegetables, and which,
I may mention, can all be used in the same way as the fresh-
grown roots and greens, except for salads—one must have
them fresh, crisp, and newly picked for that purpose.

For salads, the young pigweed is a good substitute for
lettuce, and the fresh young shoots of the rough-leaved native
fig make excellent spinach. As a rule there are far more edible
roots and plants close to the seacoast than there are farther
inland, but in every district there are some that can be utilised
by the white settlers. Whatever the blacks eat the whites
may safely try. Speaking personally, I am beholden to
the blacks for nearly all my knowledge of the different
edible ground game, recipes for the cooking of which have
been given in this and my other works on cookery. Many
people are disgusted at the mere idea of eating the white
wood grub which the blacks are so fond of. As a matter of
fact, there is nothing nasty or disgusting in these soft white
morsels, any more than there is in an oyster. It is all a
matter of taste. Both are often swallowed alike; for my own
part, I prefer the grubs parched before eating. If done over
a clear fire, on a piece of tin or a flat stone, they are delicious.
I have never tried them in a curry, but feel sure they would
be excellent. Cobera is another Bush delicacy white men very
soon acquire a taste for. There is also a large brown grass-
hopper, which is edible and very good when parched. I know
of nothing better than the tail part of a young iguana. Either
cooked on the ashes or cut up and curried, it is as nice a dish

as I would wish. Any size up to three feet they are good, but over that they may be coarse and rank, though I have eaten them when much larger and found no unpleasant taste. It all depends on the season, and the best time for iguanas is when the birds are nesting and they have been living on birds eggs and the myriads of insect life peculiar to the early spring. Carpet snake is very good roasted; unfortunately, there is not much on them.

Of the larger game, bandicoots, wallaby, and kangaroo, few people in the Bush nowadays are prejudiced against their use. I have used kangaroo and wallaby, salted and cured, the same as beef, and, save for the absence of fat, consider them almost as good; very much better than what is commonly styled "salt horse" six months old.

I would advise every housewife in the Bush to experiment and try everything; the blacks or her own common sense will soon tell her what is edible and what is not. There is a great amount of pleasure to be gained in trying new dishes with primitive materials. The Bush teems with animal life, and are we not told that the Almighty has placed it there for the benefit and sustenance of man?

Beside the food supply, there are many useful things in the Bush. The gum or resin of the grass-tree can be used in soap-making. As an instance of what can be done, I may mention that I have made excellent soap, using mangrove ashes for the lye, fish oil instead of fat, and grass-tree gum in place of resin. One would not utilise such products except under extraordinary circumstances, but many useful things have been discovered in this way, and used always afterwards. The grass-tree gum and mangrove ashes I always used in my soap-making after that. Very good varnish can be made with the gum from some of the native trees, and as for the medicinal value of many of them, they are wonderful. It may not be generally known that the chewed up leaves of the young red shoots of the gum will often stop obstinate bleeding. For a child feverish through teething or any other infantile disorder nothing is better than a hot bath in which young gum (eucalyptus) leaves have been soaked or boiled. The best way is to fill bags of mosquito net with the tender shoots and leaves, and pour the boiling water over them. I have tried this over and over again with my own children, and never found it fail. Living away in the Bush, many miles from a medical man, and with a young family subject to the usual ills that child life is liable to, I found eucalyptus leaves a sort of universal remedy. I have used it even as a poultice for wounds and gatherings, and for sore throat the steam from an infusion of young leaves always gave relief, and I believe if it was used in cases of low and colonial fever as I have described for children—viz., the bath in water the leaves have been soaked in—a cure would be effected much sooner than is usual with the ordinary remedies used. The after effects of a bath as I describe are delightful, but the leaves must be used. I have tried the extract in the water, but not with the same success. In the days when I first used these remedies eucalyptus was not so much known (if at all). I used to call them gum leaves, and got finely laughed at for my faith in them. The blacks first taught me their value, but I believe I was the first white woman who used a eucalyptus bath to reduce fever. I have wandered a long way from the subject I started with. However, my experience may be of use to mothers with little ones teething, as well as to those who are preparing food for children of an older growth.

Broiled Oysters.—*Ingredients :* $\frac{1}{2}$ a bottle of large oysters, a little cayenne, salt, butter, toast. *Mode :* Drain the oysters and dry them in a soft cloth; dust a little cayenne over each one and a little salt. Oil some butter and dip each oyster in it, then place them in a double grid-iron, the bars of which must be greased to prevent their sticking. Broil over a brisk, clear fire, basting with melted butter while cooking. Serve on hot buttered toast.

Stewed Oysters.—*Ingredients :* 1 bottle of oysters, 1 pint water, $\frac{1}{2}$ a cup of cream, 1 teaspoonful butter, pepper, salt, and bread crumbs. *Mode :* Separate the oysters from the liquor, and put the latter into a stewpan with 1 pint of water, the cream, butter, and seasoning, thicken with bread crumbs, and lastly drop the oysters in; let them cook a few minutes, and serve with snippets of toast.

To Cook Quail.—Pick these little birds very carefully, so the skin will not be torn. Split the back open to take the inside out; wash quickly, but on no account let them lie in water. Push the legs well up on the side of the breast, cut the head off close to the body, flatten them with the cleaver; salt and pepper each one, and lay them on the broiler over a clear charcoal fire. They should cook in about ten minutes. Then lay each on a slice of buttered toast and garnish with watercress. Serve with red currant or rosella jelly.

Oyster Soup.—*Ingredients:* 2 quarts oysters, a little mace, 1 stalk of celery, ½ teaspoon pepper, a dust of cayenne, ¼ pound butter, 2 tablespoonfuls flour, 1½ pints cream, 1½ pints milk. *Mode:* Strain the liquor from the oysters, salt it if necessary, and add a little mace and the celery chopped fine, the pepper and cayenne. Let it simmer over the fire a few minutes, then add the butter rubbed smooth with the flour, and the cream and milk mixed. Let it come to a boil, stirring carefully all the time. Then throw in the oysters and let them boil up once. Serve very hot. Time to make, about one hour.

Tomato Pickle.—Take 2 or 3 dozen of the small red or yellow tomatoes. Let them be ripe, but quite firm. Prick each one in two or three places, and preserve any juice that may flow from them.

Put the tomatoes into deep earthern jars in layers, and sprinkle salt—not very much—between each layer. Let them remain for three days. Then wash them well from the brine, and dry and put them into jars, and cover with vinegar which has been boiled with ½ ounce pepper, ½ ounce cloves, 1 tablespoonful mustard seed. Let the vinegar be cold before putting on the fruit, and add the juice that flowed from the fruit at first. Cover the jars closely, and the pickle will be ready for use in from three to four weeks.

To Cook Sand Eels.—*Ingredients:* Skin 2 pounds of eels, 3 small onions, 6 or 8 mushrooms, 1 glass of port wine, 1 tablespoonful parsley, pepper, salt, and a dust of nutmeg, 1 teaspoonful cornflour, ½ pint stock or broth. *Mode:* Divide the eels into pieces. Cut up the onions, peel and clean the mushrooms, and fry both in butter and a little flour. When nicely brown pour in the stock or broth, then the wine, parsley, and seasoning ; blend the cornflour and add it, then put in the pieces of eels, and let them stew very slowly till tender. Time, thirty-five to forty-five minutes.

Orange and Bread Pudding.—*Ingredients :* 2 or 3 thin slices of bread, ½ a cup of milk, 3 sweet oranges, 1 ounce butter, 3 ounces sugar, 2 eggs. *Mode :* Put the bread into a pie-dish and pour the milk over it; let it soak an hour. Grate the rinds from 3 oranges, squeeze the juice out, and remove all pips. Beat the butter with the yolks of the 2 eggs and the sugar, add these to the other ingredients, and thoroughly mix all together. Pour the orange mixture over the bread, and bake in a slow oven. Beat the whites of the eggs to a stiff froth, and a little while before serving place this roughly in bits on the pudding. Put it into the oven for a few minutes, just long enough to take a light brown. This quantity will make enough for three or four persons. Time, thirty to forty minutes to bake.

Vegetable Stew. — *Ingredients :* 1 pound of German lentils, 3 carrots, 3 turnips, 2 onions, 1 stalk celery, 3 potatoes, ½ pint milk, a little parsley, and 1 tablespoonful ketchup, dry toast. *Mode :* Soak the lentils over night. Next morning throw them into a pint of cold water, with the carrots, scraped and sliced, the turnips and onions, peeled and sliced, the celery, the potatoes, also peeled and sliced. Let all boil till tender, then add the milk to thin the stew, season with pepper and salt, the parsley and ketchup. Serve very hot, with plenty of dry toast.

A Tasty Dish. — *Ingredients :* 4 large bloaters, some vinegar (spiced), pepper, salt, 1 tablespoonful chopped parsley, a squeeze of lemon juice, and some buttered toast. *Mode :* Cut down the backs and remove the bones from 4 bloaters. Well wash the fish, then place the fillets in a pie-dish, and cover them with spiced vinegar. Let them steep in this an hour or two, then remove from the vinegar and pepper and salt them. Melt a little lard or dripping in a frying-pan, and put in the fillets. Where necessary they must be tied with thread, to keep them together. And fry till cooked; then lay each one on buttered toast, sprinkle a little parsley over and the squeeze of a lemon, and serve hot.

Cocoanut Pudding Baked.—*Ingredients :* 6 ounces of bread crumbs, a pinch of salt, half a nutmeg (grated), 2 ounces of fresh cocoanut (grated), 4 tablespoonfuls of sugar, a little lemon-peel, 3 eggs, a pint and a half of milk, 1 ounce butter. *Mode :* Put the bread crumbs into a basin with a pinch of salt, the nutmeg, cocoanut, and sugar ; grate a little lemon-peel into it, whisk the eggs with the milk, and mix into the dry ingredients ; let it stand covered over for two hours. Then beat it well with a fork, add the butter, and pour the pudding into a well-buttered pie-dish, and bake in a moderate oven. Time to bake, thirty to forty minutes.

To Cook Parsnips.—This vegetable is not generally liked, for some inexplicable reason or other. They are often boiled till tender, and then mashed with an equal quantity of potatoes. Another way is to cut them into quarters, and cut away the woody portion in the centre. Throw them into boiling water salted, let them boil quickly for about an hour, or till quite tender, then drain away the water, put into a vegetable dish, and serve with melted butter over them.

Hot-Cross Buns.—*Ingredients :* 2 pounds flour, ¼ pound butter, a little salt, ½ a cup yeast, 1 pint milk, ½ pound brown sugar, ½ a nutmeg (grated), ½ pound currants, 2 eggs, 1 packet mixed spice. *Mode :* Rub the butter into the flour and add the salt. Mix the yeast with the warm milk, and gradually stir it into the flour till it forms a light batter. Cover the basin and place it near the fire to rise, then work the sugar into it, the nutmeg, currants, spice, and the eggs well beaten. Knead these well into the dough, cover again, and leave it for another half or three-quarters of an hour near the fire, when it will be ready to make into buns; place them on buttered baking tins, make a cross on the top, brush them over with oiled butter, and bake in a moderate oven. Time, from twenty to twenty-five minutes. The above receipt is intended for brewers' yeast, which works much quicker

than home-made.   If the latter is used, the sponge must
be set over night.

Egg Sauce for Fish.—*Ingredients:* 1 tablespoonful of
flour, 3 ounces butter, about a cupful of the liquor from the
fish, 3 eggs.   *Mode:* Melt in a small saucepan 2 ounces of
the butter, add the liquor from the fish (a cupful), blend the
flour with a little water and stir it in; when on the point of
boiling, draw to one side and put in the remainder of the
butter.   Have the eggs hard-boiled, and chop them up and stir
them into the sauce; boil another minute and then it is ready.

To Cook Salt Fish.—To prepare salt fish so that it may
be tender and appetising, steep it in cold water for twenty-four
hours before using.   About an hour and a half before it is to be
served put it into a saucepan, with plenty of cold water and
about half a cup of vinegar, and let it heat very gradually;
do not allow it to boil, or it will be hard as leather.   When
on the point of boiling draw it to one side and let it simmer
for half an hour.   Drain it, and serve very hot with egg sauce.

Rhubarb Jelly.—*Ingredients:* Sufficient rhubarb to fill
a 2-quart basin, 10 ounces sugar, 1 lemon, 1 ounce gelatine.
Mode: Cut into pieces, and pare as much of the pink of the
rhubarb as will fill a 2-quart basin.   Put with it the sugar,
the thinly pared rind of the lemon, with the juice, and about
three parts of a cup of water.   Cover with a plate and
stand the basin in the oven till all the juice is extracted.
Soak the gelatine in a cupful of cold water for half an hour.
When the juice is ready strain it over the gelatine and boil
it altogether for five or six minutes in an enamelled saucepan.   Then strain again into a mould previously soaked in
cold water, let it stand till quite firm, and serve with
whipped cream.

Prawn Curry.—*Ingredients:* Some fresh prawns, peeled,
—or a tin of preserved,—$\frac{1}{2}$ a cocoanut, grated, 1 onion, some
white stock or milk, 2 teaspoonfuls of curry powder, 1 tablespoonful flour, 1 lemon.   *Mode:* Peel the prawns and stew
them in a little water till tender.   Grate or rasp $\frac{1}{2}$ a cocoanut into about $\frac{1}{2}$ a cup of hot water, and pass it through a

sieve. Shred up a small onion and add it to the prawns. Strain off some of the water from them, and add about a cup of white stock or sweet milk. Season with pepper, salt, and a dust of cinnamon, if liked. Let this stew a few minutes, then blend the curry powder and flour into a paste with the milk of the cocoanut, and stir it into the saucepan. Also add the strained cocoanut. Let the whole simmer for about ten minutes. Serve with rice piled round the dish.

Orange Cream. — *Ingredients :* 1 ounce isinglass or gelatine, 6 oranges, 1 lemon, 6 ounces of loaf sugar, 1 small cup of cream, and the same of milk. *Mode :* Soak the isinglass or gelatine in less than $\frac{1}{2}$ a pint of cold water for an hour, then pour over it $\frac{1}{2}$ a pint of boiling water, add the juice of the oranges and the 1 lemon—the sugar previously rubbed on the rind of the oranges. Pour this into a saucepan, and stir it gently over the fire for ten minutes or so. Strain it into a basin, and when nearly cold beat into it the cream and the milk. Beat the mixture for some time, and then pour it into a wet mould and let it stand on ice, if possible, till next day. Then turn on to a glass dish.

Cauliflower Pudding.—*Ingredients :* 1 cauliflower, 3 or 4 slices of bacon, 3 tablespoonfuls minced veal or mutton, 4 tablespoonfuls bread crumbs, 3 tablespoonfuls beef suet, 1 teaspoonful chopped parsley, 3 eggs, $\frac{1}{2}$ cup of good gravy or stock. *Mode :* Boil the cauliflower in salt and water for fifteen minutes, then drain it well, and cut off the stalk and green part, and separate the flower into sprigs. Line the sides and bottom of a pudding basin with slices of bacon, and closely pack in the sprigs of cauliflower stalk upwards, and fill in the spaces with the stuffing made with the bread crumbs, minced meat, suet, and herbs ; season well with pepper and salt. Place another layer of cauliflower, then more stuffing till the basin is filled, then beat up the eggs and gravy together, and pour it over the whole. Cover the basin with a plate and bake in a moderate oven. When done, turn out on to a hot dish and serve. Time to bake, about one hour.

Preserved Rhubarb.—Take some stalks of young rhubarb, the thickest you can get, pare it, and cut into lengths of about two inches. Weigh it, and lay in plates in single layers, and cover with good loaf sugar (allowing 1 pound to 1 pound of rhubarb), and the grated rind of 3 or 4 lemons. Let this stand twenty-four hours. Then make a strong syrup with 1 pound sugar to 1 cup water, boil for ten minutes, and add the syrup from the rhubarb and a little grated ginger. Let this boil up, then throw in the bits of rhubarb, and let them simmer till tender. Remove them carefully into jars; allow the syrup to boil for another ten minutes, and pour it over the rhubarb. When cold cover the jars, and store away in a cool, dry place for use.

Mayonnaise Sauce.—This very delicious dressing for salads can be kept in stock for some little time, and as it takes both time and patience to mix properly, it is always as well to have it ready, in case a salad be required in a hurry. Everything depends on the mixing, which cannot be done without patience and care. *Mode :* Break the yolk of a fresh egg into a bowl, and beat it with a wooden spoon, adding 1 teaspoonful of salt and half the amount of pepper. When it is thick, add, drop by drop, and stirring all the time, 2 tablespoonfuls of good Lucca oil, and 1 tablespoonful of white vinegar, also 5 drops of lemon juice, which will give it a creamy look. Continue adding oil, vinegar and lemon juice in this way till a pint of oil with vinegar in proportion has been used; then bottle and cork for use when required.

Rice Cake.—*Ingredients :* $\frac{1}{4}$ pound flour, $\frac{1}{4}$ pound ground rice, $\frac{1}{4}$ pound sugar, $\frac{1}{4}$ pound butter, 2 eggs, $\frac{1}{2}$ teaspoonful essence of lemon, $\frac{1}{2}$ teacupful milk, $\frac{1}{2}$ teaspoonful baking-powder. *Mode :* Put the butter and sugar into a basin, and beat to a cream. Add the yolks of the eggs one by one, beating as each goes in; then the milk. Beat the whites to a stiff froth. Mix the flour, ground rice, and baking-powder together, and add them by degrees to the mixture; lastly, stir in the whites and essence. Mix thoroughly and pour into a well-greased cake tin, and bake in a moderate oven. Time, from thirty to forty minutes.

Hurry-Scurry Cake.—*Ingredients :* 1 cup flour, 1 cup sugar, $\frac{1}{2}$ cup milk, $\frac{1}{2}$ small teaspoon baking soda, $\frac{1}{4}$ small teaspoon cream of tartar, 2 teaspoons marmalade, 1 egg. *Mode* : Mix all the dry things together—being careful to crush the soda with the blade of a knife—stir in the marmalade, the milk, and the egg well beaten. Grease a soup plate, put in the mixture, flatten the top and brush over with a little milk and a dust of sugar. Bake in a hot oven. Time, from twenty to twenty-five minutes.

Shortbread.—*Ingredients :* 1 pound flour, $\frac{1}{2}$ pound butter, $\frac{1}{2}$ pound good white sugar, a little candied peel. *Mode* : Mix the sugar and butter together (with the hands is best), and gradually add the flour, kneading well, and keeping the lump firm. When all is worked into a stiff paste, cut it into two or three pieces, make each piece round or oval, as desired, and about half an inch thick, pinch the edges, prick them over with a fork, put some slips of candied peel on top, and bake in a slow oven till they are a nice brown.

To Pickle Ham and Bacon.—Pack the meat in a sweet, clean cask, and cover with brine made as follows :—Take half as much water as will cover the meat, and add to it all the salt it will dissolve, fill in the other half of the water required, with 4 pints of molasses and $\frac{1}{4}$ pound of saltpetre for every 100 pounds of meat. Leave the meat in this for six weeks, and then smoke it. In warm weather the smoke-house should be as dark as possible, to guard against flies. As soon as the meat is sufficiently smoked—which is all a matter of taste—each piece should be wrapped in a paper bag, securely fastened, so no insect can get through to it, and then hung in a dry place. If these directions are properly carried out the hams and bacon should keep almost any time.

To Cook Parrots.—*Ingredients :* One dozen parrots, 1 ounce butter, and 1 ounce flour, $\frac{1}{2}$ pint milk, seasoning of pepper, salt and nutmeg, 1 tablespoonful of chopped parsley, a little stock. *Mode* : Mix the butter and the flour smoothly in a stewpan over a moderate fire. Gradually add the milk and seasoning. Stir the sauce till it boils, then pour in as much stock as will make it sufficient for the birds. Put in the parrots, well-picked and cleaned, and let them stew, closely covered until they are tender. Add a little extra milk or stock if it boils away much. About five minutes before serving sprinkle in the chopped parsley. Serve very hot, with the sauce poured round the birds. Time, from thirty to forty minutes to cook.

Peach Snowballs.—*Ingredients:* 1 pound of rice, some sugar, 6 peaches. *Mode:* Throw the rice into a saucepan of boiling water and let it boil from five to seven minutes. Drain it, and when it has cooled spread it in equal parts on six small pudding cloths. Peel the peaches carefully, coat them thickly with sugar and place one in the centre of each layer of rice ; gather the cloth round and securely tie it. Then plunge these puddings into boiling water, and when done turn them out, sprinkle with sugar, and serve with a sweet sauce over them. Time, one hour and a half to boil.

Orange Sauce.—*Ingredients:* 1 large orange, 3 or 4 lumps of sugar, 2 teaspoonfuls of cornflour, 1 teaspoonful butter, 1 cup milk, 1 tablespoonful white sugar. *Mode:* Rub the lumps of sugar upon the rind of the orange till most of the yellow is removed. Scrape out the pulp, or orange part, removing pips and skin, and add it to the sugar. Blend the cornflour with a little water, add the butter, the spoonful of sugar and the milk. Stir over the fire till the sauce thickens, then strain, and serve either in a boat or over the pudding.

To Cook an Ox-cheek. — *Ingredients:* A moderate-sized ox-cheek, 1 tablespoonful salt, 1 teaspoonful pepper. 2 stalks celery, 2 onions, 2 turnips, 2 carrots, 3 tablespoonfuls cornflour or ground rice, a little sauce or mushroom ketchup. *Mode:* Wash the cheek carefully, and soak it in cold salt and water for five or six hours. After which drain it and sprinkle with a tablespoonful of salt and the pepper. Put it into a large saucepan, with about 3 quarts of cold water, the celery, onions, etc., and when it begins to boil remove the scum that rises, draw the saucepan to the side of the fire and simmer the contents gently for three hours. Mix the cornflour or ground rice with a little water and the sauce or ketchup ; add this to the broth, and boil another half-hour. Serve the ox-cheek with the vegetables round it, and the broth makes excellent soup. Time, three hours and a half.

Carrot Jam.—The deep coloured carrot is the best for preserving. Wash and scrape them, and put into a potato steamer till tender. When cold, pulp them first with a masher, then through a sieve, and to every 1 pound of pulp allow 10 ounces of sugar. and the juice of 1 lemon, and to every 4 pound, the grated rind of 1 lemon; more of the rind will make it too bitter. Ginger can be boiled with it if preferred, or 2 or 3 tablespoonfuls of the essence added when done. Let the jam cook slowly till it becomes clear. Sometimes a little water is added when the sugar is put in; it is all a matter of judgment. Sometimes there is sufficient moisture in the carrots to make juice, sometimes not, and then it may be necessary to allow a pint or two of water.

Fish Cakes.—*Ingredients:* Any cold fish, some cooked potatoes, 1 tablespoonful butter, salt, pepper, 2 eggs, some fine bread crumbs, dripping to fry. *Mode:* Free the fish from all skin and bones, put it into a basin with an equal quantity of cold potatoes, and mash the whole together with the potato-masher. One pound of fish and potatoes mixed will make a good dish. Add the butter, when the mixture is quite smooth, the seasoning and 1 egg. Mould into small flat cakes, dip in egg, and cover with bread crumbs. Fry in plenty of boiling fat. Arrange on a napkin, and garnish with parsley or pickled eggs.

Ox-cheek Stewed.—*Ingredients:* Half a cheek, 1 tablespoonful each of suet, parsley, thyme, 1 cup fine bread crumbs, 2 eggs, seasoning of salt and pepper, vegetables if liked. *Mode:* This is rather a troublesome dish, and should be, if possible, partly cooked the previous day. Be sure that the cheek is fresh, also that the butcher removes the internal cartilage of the nostrils, the eye and jawbones. Steep it all night in salt and water; wash well and drain. Put into a large saucepan with plenty of cold water and salt; when it boils, skim well, and when it has boiled hard twenty minutes, or half an hour, take it out, throw away that water, and return it to the saucepan in fresh hot water. Now boil for about three hours and remove. Take away the bones and trim into shape. Put into a stewpan, and cover with the suet,

E

herbs and bread crumbs, pour in sufficient of the liquor it was boiled in to cover it, add the eggs beaten up, and simmer very gently till quite tender. A few vegetables may be boiled with it if liked. And it can be served either hot or cold, with the gravy thickened.

To Preserve Cumquats.—Pick the fruit free from all stalks, and throw them into strong salt and water. Let them soak two or three days in this, then boil in fresh water till the skin can be pierced with a straw ; do not let the fruit break if possible, drain them, and when cold pierce each cumquat in several places with a straw or a large bonnet pin. Make a strong syrup, of 2 cups sugar to 1 cup water. About 3 cups water to 6 of sugar should be enough to cover 12 dozen cumquats, or if necessary make a little more, but on no account have too much syrup. Boil the sugar and water together, and skim it. Throw in the fruit and let them boil five minutes. Remove from the fire into a deep basin, and let them stand two days, then pour off the syrup and reboil it with 2 cups more sugar. When boiling, pour over the fruit. A large washhand-stand jug is one of the best receptacles for the fruit at this stage. Let them stand again two days, and repeat the boiling, making the syrup stronger each time. Do this four or five times, the last time putting the fruit into the jars and pouring the syrup over them. Tie down, and store away for a week or two, when they will be fit for use.

Good Pickle for Beef.—When beef is pickled in too much salt it becomes dry and hard when boiled, and loses much of its nourishment. The following is one of the best pickles I know of for use in the Bush, where "killing day" does not come every week. *Ingredients :* To 12 gallons water, 8 pounds salt, 4 pounds brown sugar, $\frac{1}{2}$ pound baking soda, 3 ounces saltpetre, and 4 ounces black, or, if liked, 2 ounces cayenne. *Mode :* Boil the above ingredients together, skim carefully and let it cool, then pour over the beef. In two weeks, or sooner in summer, pour off the brine and boil it again, as it will have become bloody. Skim it, and when cold pour over the beef. If it should again become bloody, repeat the boiling and skimming ; but, as a rule, the second is sufficient. This makes excellent sweetmeat, and will keep a length of time. The best of corned beef may be spoilt in the boiling. The great secret is to use a large quantity of water, and to fill up the saucepan as it boils away. If the meat is to be used cold, let it cool in the water.

Hop Beer.—*Ingredients:* 4 gallons water, 10 pounds sugar, 4 ounces hops, $\frac{1}{2}$ packet isinglass, $\frac{1}{3}$ pound raisins, and 1 pint of yeast or 2 large bottles of porter. *Mode:* Boil the sugar and hops with 4 gallons of water for one hour and a half. Strain into a cask, through muslin, and add 6 gallons more water. Pour in the yeast and the raisins, and let it work for five days. On the fourth day add the isinglass, dissolved in a little of the beer. Then it is ready for bottling.

Walnut Cakes.—*Ingredients:* Half a pound sifted flour, 2 ounces butter, whites of 4 eggs, 3 ounces walnuts, $\frac{1}{2}$ teaspoon baking powder, 1 teaspoon vanilla. *Mode:* Beat the butter and sugar to a cream, add the sifted flour and the baking powder, mix well, then stir in the walnuts, chopped up fine, lastly the whites of the eggs, well beaten, and the vanilla essence. Drop on to a slide and bake in a moderate oven.

Oatmeal Drink.—*Ingredients:* 3 tablespoons oatmeal, 3 quarts water, sugar to taste, some thin lemon-peel, flavour with lemon juice or anything else preferred. *Mode:* Put the oatmeal into the cold water and boil it half an hour with the thinly pared lemon-peel. Remove from the fire and sweeten. When cold add the lemon juice or other flavouring. Rice or barley drink can be made the same way, using broken rice or barley instead of oatmeal.

Tomato Preserve.—*Ingredients:* Small green tomatoes are the best to use, the kind that do not ripen readily. Take 4 pounds of tomatoes, 3 pounds white sugar, 3 lemons, some whole ginger. *Mode:* Remove the stems from the fruit, put them into a preserving pan with water to cover them (barely); boil in this for a little while without breaking them. Remove and drain them. Then make a strong syrup of 2 cups sugar to 1 of water, and having pricked all the tomatoes with a pin in several places, drop them into the syrup and boil a few minutes. Remove and let them stand till cold. Shred up the lemons and boil in water till the skin is tender. Strain the syrup from the tomatoes and boil it again with the lemon. Pour over the tomatoes, and let them stand two days; then strain, boil, and pour over the fruit a third time. Repeat twice more, and then bottle, tie down, and store away for a month before eating.

To stew Eels.—*Ingredients :* 1 or 2 eels, cold water, salt, chopped parsley, 1 tablespoon butter and a little flour. *Mode :* Skin and clean the eels, take out all fat from the inside. Cut into lengths about two inches long, put into a stewpan with sufficient water to cover them; add salt, pepper, and some chopped parsley. Stew very slowly, closely covered, for an hour. At the last add the butter and a little flour, blended with cold water. Serve in a deep dish and very hot.

Rice Fritters.—*Ingredients :* 2 ounces of rice, boiled in milk and water, 1 ounce sugar, 1 tablespoonful flour, 2 eggs, a few currants, some essence of almonds, and milk. *Mode :* Boil the rice till quite soft in milk and water. Let it cool, and mix in the sugar, the currants, well washed, the flour, and the eggs, well beaten ; add a few drops of essence of almonds, and a little milk to make it the right consistency ; drop the mixture from a tablespoon into boiling fat, and fry a light brown. Serve very hot with sugar over them.

Good plain Cake.—*Ingredients :* ½ a pound of butter or beef dripping, 1 pound sugar, 3 eggs, ½ pint milk, 1 pound flour, ¼ pound sweet almonds, ½ pound currants, 3 ounces candied peel. *Mode :* Beat the butter to a cream and mix in the sugar. Beat up the eggs, mix them with the milk and stir into the butter. Then add the flour, the almonds blanched and chopped small, the currants and candied peel. Beat all well together. Bake in a well-greased tin for about one and a half hours.

Rosella Pickle.—*Ingredients :* Rosellas, vinegar, spice, peppercorns, chillies, salt and water. *Mode :* Peel the fruit from the seed-pod in as large pieces as possible. Throw them into salted water for five or six hours. Then boil the vinegar with some whole spice, peppercorns and bird's-eye chillies.

Put the fruit into jars or bottles and pour the vinegar over it when cool. Tie down and store away for a week or two.

Home-made extract of Malt.—Get half a bushel of ground malt, and pour over it as much *hot* (but not boiling) water as will cover it ; let it stand for forty-eight hours, then strain the liquor off clear without disturbing the malt grains. Put this liquor into a large preserving pan, so there will be plenty of room to boil it quickly without it boiling over. When it begins to thicken stir constantly, and boil till it is as thick as treacle. When cool bottle it for use.

This is an excellent tonic for delicate children, or, indeed, for any one who suffers from chest or throat complaints.

Extract of malt is expensive if one buys it at the chemist's, but the above recipe, if properly carried out, will answer just as well as the best the chemists can sell, and cost less— a consideration if several in a family are ordered the tonic.

Cook's Scales.—10 ordinary-sized eggs weigh 1 pound.
Soft butter the size of an egg weighs 1 ounce.
1 quart of sifted flour (well heaped) weighs 1 pound.
1 pint of sugar weighs 13 ounces.
2 teacups (well heaped) of coffee weigh 1 pound.
2 teacups of soft butter (well packed) weigh 1 pound.
1⅓ pints of powdered sugar weighs 1 pound.
2 tablespoonfuls of powdered sugar or flour weigh 1 ounce.
1 tablespoonful (well rounded) of soft butter weighs 1 ounce.

To preserve Apricots.—Take about 4 pounds of apricots just before they are fully ripe. Gather them early in the morning if possible ; make a little slit with a knife at the stalk end and work the stone out. Throw them into cold water, and simmer gently till they are soft enough for a pin to be pushed through them. Take them out and put them into fresh cold water. Now make a syrup of 4 pounds sugar and 1 quart water ; stir till the sugar is dissolved, and boil over a slow fire, skim well, adding every now and then a table-spoonful of cold water to make the scum rise. Remove from the fire, drain the fruit and put them into the syrup, and let them stand till it is nearly cold, then put on to the fire again and boil for five minutes. Do this three or four times, and the last time let it boil till the fruit is quite clear, which should be in fifteen or twenty minutes. Just before taking from the fire blanch a few of the kernels and add them.

Clove Cordial.—*Ingredients:* 2 ounces of cloves, 16 ounces rectified spirit. *Mode:* Macerate these for ten or twelve days. Then strain through thick muslin or linen. Express the residuum strongly to obtain the last of the fluid. Do the macerating in a stone jar, and shake well two or three times each day.

Sherbet.—*Ingredients:* 8 ounces sugar, 4 ounces tartaric acid, 4 ounces carbonate of soda, 30 drops essence of lemon. *Mode:* Mix the ingredients dry, having first pounded each separately, and then altogether. Put into a wide-necked bottle and keep well corked. A small teaspoonful stirred into a glass of water makes a wholesome and pleasant summer drink.

Plain Tea Cake.—*Ingredients:* ½ pound of butter, ½ pound sugar, 1 pound flour, 2 teaspoonfuls baking powder, ½ pound currants, sufficient milk to moisten. *Mode:* Beat the butter and sugar together. Mix the baking-powder in with the flour, and add it by degrees, then the currants. Moisten with milk and bake in a moderate oven. Time, about forty minutes.

Spice Cake.—*Ingredients:* ¾ pound flour, ½ pound currants, ½ pound sultanas, ¼ pound candied peel, ¼ pound butter, ¼ pound sugar, 2 teaspoonfuls of spice, ½ nutmeg, grated, 1 teaspoonful ginger, 2 teaspoonfuls baking-powder, 2 eggs, a little milk. *Mode:* Rub the butter into the flour, then add the spices, baking-powder, sugar, and then the fruit and candied peel. Beat up the eggs with some milk, stir it in and beat all together till everything is thoroughly well mixed. Pour into a well-buttered tin and bake. Time, about one hour.

Chocolate Macaroons.—*Ingredients:* ½ pound of Valencia almonds, ¼ pound powdered or icing sugar, ¼ pound chocolate powder, whites of 2 or 3 eggs. *Mode:* Blanch, peel, and pound the almonds in a mortar till reduced to a paste, add the sugar by degrees and then the chocolate. It is best to buy the chocolate in squares or cakes and grate them on a fine grater. Whisk the whites to a stiff froth, and work the ingredients into a paste with them. Spread a sheet of white paper on the baking-tin, and drop the mixture on to it from a spoon, and bake in a very cool oven for a few minutes.

Cocoanut Sweets.—*Ingredients:* 2 ounces of cocoanut, whites of 2 eggs, ¼ pound powdered sugar. *Mode:* Grate the cocoanut and roll in a cloth to absorb the moisture; beat the whites of 2 eggs to a stiff froth, stir in the sugar and cocoanut, drop the mixture on to white paper in little pyramid shapes, place in a cool oven and leave them till they are crisp.

Shortbread.—*Ingredients:* 1 pound butter, ½ pound sugar, ¾ pound flour, 4 ounces ground rice. *Mode:* Beat the butter to a cream with the sugar, stir in the flour and ground rice, and work the whole into a stiff paste. Roll out to about a quarter of an inch in thickness and cut into biscuits. Bake on a tin lined with white paper.

Ratifia Biscuits.—*Ingredients:* 4 ounces of sweet almonds, 1 pound powdered sugar, 1 ounce ground rice, whites of 2 or 3 eggs. *Mode:* Blanch, peel, and pound the almonds in a mortar with the sugar and ground rice. Whisk the whites of the eggs and with them work the mixture into a paste. Drop from the spoon on to white paper, and bake in a cool oven until they are crisp.

Wine Biscuits.—*Ingredients:* ½ pound of butter, ½ pound sugar, 3 eggs, 1½ pounds flour, a few drops of sal volatile. *Mode:* Beat the butter to a cream with the sugar. Then drop the eggs in one at a time and beat the mixture well, then stir in quickly the flour, add the sal volatile; roll the paste out and cut into thin biscuits. Bake in a quick oven for about ten or fifteen minutes.

Good Stimulant for an Invalid.—*Ingredients:* 1 pint of new milk, 1 cup cream, yolks of 2 eggs, ½ ounce Swinborne's isinglass sugar, 2 wine-glasses of good brandy. *Mode:* Beat the milk, cream, and eggs together for a few minutes, sweeten to taste, then dissolve the isinglass in a little hot water, and add it and the brandy. Divide the quantity, and give half before rising in the morning and the other half when going to bed. This is excellent in cases of great debility, and with consumptive patients, if given before rising in the morning, will often stave off a fit of coughing while dressing.

A Luncheon Pudding.—*Ingredients:* ½ an ounce of gelatine, ½ pint boiling water, 1 pint cream or milk, 1 pot raspberry or rosella jelly, 3 ounces loaf sugar, juice of 1 lemon. *Mode:* Soak the gelatine an hour or so, then dissolve it in the boiling water. Add the cream or milk, stir in the jelly, the sugar and lemon juice, and whisk altogether till it thickens. Pour into a wet mould and stand in some freezing mixture.

Shrimp Salad.—*Ingredients:* ¼ of a pound of good mellow cheese, 1 teaspoonful made mustard, 1 tablespoonful salad oil or oiled butter, 1 tablespoonful vinegar, 1 teaspoonful sugar, salt and pepper, 1 lettuce and some shrimps. *Mode:* Wash and pick some fresh young lettuce, and shred part for the salad bowl and leave some of the tenderest leaves and heart whole. Pound the cheese in a mortar, and mix with it the mustard, the oil (by degrees), the sugar, salt, pepper and vinegar, making it the consistency of cream. Add a little cream or milk if necessary. Pour this over the lettuce in the salad bowl. Arrange little heaps of freshly picked shrimps and the leaves and heart of the lettuce round the bowl, and serve.

If preferred, the shrimps can be chopped up small and mixed in with the dressing.

Celery Salad.—*Ingredients:* The tenderest stalks of 3 heads of celery, yolks of 2 hard-boiled eggs, 3 tablespoonfuls salad oil, 1 tablespoonful vinegar, ½ teaspoonful dry mustard, pepper and salt, cream. *Mode:* Cut the celery into strips, an inch or so long, much the same as one cuts French beans. Rub the salad bowl with an eschalot. Mix the yolks of the eggs with the oil by degrees, almost drop by drop, add the mustard, pepper, salt, and then the vinegar. At the last pour about half a cup of cream over the celery, and then add the sauce. Garnish with the whites of the eggs, and serve with chopped mushrooms.

Beef-Grenadins.—*Ingredients:* Rump steak, some fat bacon, butter, pepper and salt, some good stock. *Mode:* Cut some rump-steak in slices, about half an inch thick, trim them to the same size and shape, lard them thickly on one side with fat bacon. Lay them in a saucepan, the larded side undermost, with some butter, and fry them till the bacon takes colour. Turn them over, season with pepper and salt, and fry again on that side. Then pour in a little good 'stock, let it come to the boil, and thicken with a little browned flour. Dish the grenadines round a centre of brussels sprouts, or any green vegetables.

Bigarade Sauce.—*Ingredients:* The thin rind of 2 oranges, butter, flour, a little stock, pepper, salt, and a pinch of sugar, the juice of the oranges. *Mode:* Pare off the rind as thinly as possible, or grate it from 2 Seville oranges; cut into very thin shreds and boil in water a few minutes. Melt a tablespoonful of butter in a saucepan, stir into it gradually a tablespoonful of flour till it begins to colour. Add half a cup of stock, pepper, salt, and the sugar, then put in the rinds, stir till the sauce boils, add the juice from the oranges, and serve with roast wild duck, etc.

Sago and Rice Pudding.—*Ingredients:* 2 tablespoonfuls each of rice and sago, 2 cups milk, 2 tablespoons sugar, any flavouring liked. *Mode:* Soak the rice and sago in the milk for two hours, add the sugar, stir well till it has dissolved, butter a pie-dish, and pour the milk, etc., into it, stir in the flavouring, and bake in a slow oven an hour or a little longer.

Small Black Cap Pudding.—*Ingredients:* A tablespoonful butter, 2 tablespoons flour, ¾ cup milk, sugar to taste, 3 eggs, a handful of currants. *Mode:* Put the butter into a small stewpan, and when melted stir in the flour smoothly, but do not let it brown. Add the milk, and stir till it boils, sweeten to taste, and remove from the fire; beat the yolks and stir them in, then the whites, whisked to a stiff froth. Butter a basin, sprinkle some well-washed currants in the bottom of it, pour in the batter, and steam for twenty to thirty minutes.

Baked Apple Pudding. — *Ingredients :* 1 pound apples, ¼ pound each of sugar, bread crumbs, and butter, 3 eggs, peel, and half the juice of 1 lemon. *Mode :* Pare, core, and slice the apples in very thin slices. Butter a pie-dish, and put a layer of bread crumbs at the bottom, then a layer of apples, some pieces of butter, the grated rind of the lemon and sugar ; do this till the dish is full ; have bread crumbs on top, and pieces of butter here and there ; then beat up the eggs, and pour it over all with a spoon, so that the whole of the top gets moistened. Bake three-quarters of an hour, and turn on to a dish.

To fry Fish.—Cut the pieces moderately thick, and if the fish is a large one take out the backbone. Wash each piece carefully, sprinkle with salt, and lay in a dry cloth for a few minutes. Beat up an egg, dip each piece of fish in it, then into flour quickly, and transfer to the pan of boiling *oil* (not dripping). Do not turn till one side is quite done. If there is sufficient oil in the pan, there will be no danger of burning. Drain on kitchen paper, and serve on a folded napkin.

Collared Brawn.—*Ingredients :* Head and feet of a pig, 1 ox-tongue, 2 pounds lean beef, salt, saltpetre, pepper. *Mode :* Obtain from the butcher the head and feet of a pig, an ox-tongue, and 2 pounds of beef, and pickle them yourself by rubbing well with salt and saltpetre every day for a week or ten days. Then put on to boil for five or six hours, or till the meat comes clean off the bones ; now pick and mince the head, feet, and the beef, adding pepper to taste ; skin the tongue and put it in the middle, using a cake-tin or can with holes in the bottom, arrange the rest round it, pour in enough liquor just to moisten, put a heavy weight on to press it, and leave twelve hours.

Dough Nuts.—*Ingredients :* 3 cups flour, 3 teaspoonfuls baking-powder, ½ teaspoon salt, water to make a batter. *Mode :* Mix the flour and baking-powder together, add the salt, and pour in sufficient water to make a thick batter. Have a pan of boiling fat, and drop in from the spoon enough

of the batter to make the nuts the size of an egg. Fry for
ten minutes or till a light brown. These are very good for
breakfast, eaten with butter.

Home-made Vermicelli.—*Ingredients :* Yolks of 4 eggs,
whites of 1, pinch of salt, a little water, and as much sifted
flour as will make a very stiff paste. *Mode :* Make a paste or
dough with the eggs, salt, flour, and about a tablespoonful of
water. Work it slowly, adding the flour by degrees, and be
sure it is quite smooth. Then roll out in sheets as thinly as
possible without breaking, hang these sheets over a dry cloth
in the sun for a few minutes; do not let them dry. Then take
a sharp knife and cut into strips, or stamp in lozenges, if
liked. In an hour's time the vermicelli is ready to use, either
in soup or dressed with cheese.

Potatoes and Onions.—*Ingredients :* Equal quantities
of ready-boiled onions and potatoes, 1 tablespoonful butter,
pepper, salt, and a little milk or cream. *Mode :* Take equal
parts of onions and potatoes, mash them, and pass through a
sieve ; then put them into a saucepan with the butter, seasoning and the milk or cream. Stir well, and as soon as the
mixture is quite hot it is ready to serve.

Tapioca Custard.—*Ingredients :* 2 large tablespoonfuls
tapioca, 1 pint milk, 2 ounces sugar, 1 teaspoonful butter, 4
eggs, some stewed fruit, juice of ½ a lemon, nutmeg. *Mode :*
Wash the tapioca, and put it into a saucepan with the milk,
let it stand to steep for an hour or two, then put it by the
fire, where it will cook very, very slowly, stirring now and
then, until the tapioca is quite soft, clean, and glutinous. If
cooked quickly, it will become hard, tough, and unfit to eat.
Add more milk, if necessary, as it boils away. When quite
cooked, add the sugar and butter, and draw the saucepan off
the fire. Beat up the eggs in a basin, and pour the tapioca
and milk over them, stirring all the while. Return to the
saucepan, and stir over the fire till the eggs are cooked; but
do not let it boil, or they will curdle. Pour into a basin and
set away to cool. Put a layer of stewed fruit into a deep
glass dish, squeeze the lemon over it, and pour in the tapioca,
grate nutmeg over the top, and serve when quite cold,

Timbales, and how to make them.—Timbales, or, as they are more often called by cooks, thimbles, are small cups made of macaroni, of paste of bread, or batter, to hold some daintily prepared meat or fish. The simplest way to make them is with an iron, made for the purpose, or any iron with a knob at the end—a poker, for instance, would do. Having washed it quite clean, dip the knob into a thick batter, then quickly into the boiling fat. In a few minutes remove it, and the little cup of batter will slip off; and there you have a little crisp cup, ready to be filled with any dainty meat you choose.

Another way to make these little cups is with boiled macaroni, using a small tin cup to mould the macaroni on and white of egg to stick it together. They are also made of chicken. Chop fine the uncooked meat of a couple of chickens, put it through the mincing machine or pound in a mortar. There should be a cup of meat.

Put into a stewpan 1 cup cream, ½ cup bread crumbs, and cook for fifteen minutes. Strain this through a sieve, and add the pounded meat, and three tablespoonfuls butter, a little salt, pepper, and, lastly, the whites of 2 eggs beaten stiff. Mix these ingredients together thoroughly, and when quite cold, line buttered cups evenly and carefully, leaving no hole or space where they may break when filled. For a filling for these cups stew the remainder of the chickens; then cut the meat from the bones, and chop it fine; make a sauce by boiling half a cup of milk and 1 teaspoonful of flour together, season with salt, pepper, and a few mushrooms, if to be got. Let the chicken cook in this sauce for four or five minutes, fill the lined moulds, and set the cups in a pan of water in the oven, where the heat will be moderate; bake for half an hour.

The Batter Thimbles, or, Timbales, are much more easily made.

For the batter take ½ pint flour, ½ cup milk, 2 eggs, salt, and 1 tablespoonful salad oil. And when the shells or cups are made, fill them with chicken, fish, lobster, or any delicate meat, heated in a sauce or cream. They are very nice for a supper party or luncheon, and make a very pretty dish.

Tomato Soup.—*Ingredients :* Tomatoes, 1 pound, ham or

lean bacon, ¼ pound, 4 tablespoonfuls cornflour, 2 tablespoonfuls butter, 1 onion, 2 teaspoonfuls sugar, salt, pepper. *Mode:* Put the tomatoes into a saucepan—previously having cut them across—with 2 pints of water, the ham, onion, salt, pepper. Cover the saucepan, and cook for half an hour, then strain through a sieve. Return the soup to the saucepan, blend the cornflour, and add it when the soup is boiling, stir till it thickens, then add the sugar and butter. Serve with fried croûtons, like for pease soup.

Sage and Onion Stuffing.—*Ingredients:* Onions, 4 tablespoonfuls sage, 1 tablespoonful flour, 2 tablespoonfuls stale bread crumbs, 1 tablespoonful suet or dripping, 1 or 2 eggs, salt, and pepper. *Mode:* Parboil the onions, and chop then very fine, parch or dry the sage in the oven, or on top of the stove, crush and crumble it in the hands, and mix with the onion, add the bread crumbs, flour, dripping, seasoning, and moisten with the eggs. The best way to mix stuffing is in a basin, and break the eggs into it, without any beating, and stir with a fork till all is moistened. For roast duck, goose, pork, etc., etc.

Custard Souffles.—*Ingredients:* 2 tablespoonfuls flour, 2 tablespoonfuls butter, 2 tablespoonfuls sugar, 1 cup milk, 4 eggs. *Mode:* Put the milk on to boil, blend the flour with a little cold milk and the butter, and stir them into the boiling milk (off the fire). Cook for five minutes, stirring all the time. Beat up the yolks and sugar together, and add then to the mixture; set away to cool. Then whisk up the whites, stir them in quickly, and beat all together, pour into a soufflé, or pie-dish, and bake in a moderate oven about twenty-five minutes. Serve with a sweet sauce.

About Souffles.—Souffles and omelets may be classed in much the same category, having many similar characteristics. Neither will bear keeping when made, both are made of eggs, and both are more of a *bonne bouche*, or tit-bit, than anything else. At least, one would hardly put either in front of a very hungry man. Of the two, the soufflé is the most delicate, and requires a light hand, but there is nothing difficult or intricate in the making of a souflé, any ordinary plain cook

could make one ; the fault, when there is failure, invariably
lies with those who are to eat it, through their lingering too
long over the previous courses, and thus the soufflé, timed to
be ready to within a few minutes, *"falls"* and becomes
leathery. The correct thing is to wait for the soufflé, do not
let it wait for you. Unless served immediately it is done, it
is really not eatable ; therefore, when a mistress orders a
soufflé for dinner, she should give the signal when it is to be
put into the oven.

Baked Fish.—*Ingredients:* A piece of any large fish, or a
whole fish, if preferred, 1 tablespoonful butter, 1 teaspoonful
Worcestershire sauce, browned flour, to thicken with, 1 lemon.
Mode : About 4 pounds will be sufficient to do for a dinner
for several. Lay the fish in salt and water for an hour or
two ; then wipe dry and bake in a moderate oven for one
hour, basting frequently with hot water in which the butter
has been melted. When done it should be nicely browned.
Add to the gravy 1 teaspoonful of sauce, juice of 1 lemon, and
thicken with browned flour, and serve in a gravy dish.

Brawn of Pig's Head.—*Ingredients :* One pig's head,
savoury herbs, 1 onion, mace, pepper, salt. *Mode :* Lay the
head in salt and water for some hours, then put on to boil
in cold water. Simmer very slowly until the meat is loose
from the bone. Take it out and cut into small pieces. Put
some of the liquor it was boiled in into a saucepan with a
bunch of herbs, the onion, a little mace, pepper and salt ;
boil well, and then strain over the meat. Boil all together
again a few minutes, and then pour into a mould. Stand away
to cool with a heavy weight on top.

Reception Day Cake.—*Ingredients:* 2½ pounds flour,
1½ pounds butter, 2 pounds currants, 1 pound sultanas, 1
pound sugar, 1 nutmeg, grated, a pinch of mace and cloves, 7
or 8 eggs, ½ pound sweet almonds, ½ pound mixed peel, 1 glass
brandy, 1 glass sherry. *Mode :* Rub the butter into the flour,
mix in by degrees, all the dry ingredients and the almonds
blanched and pounded, then the eggs well beaten, and, lastly,
the wine and brandy. Line a tin with buttered paper, pour

in the mixture, and bake in a moderate oven. Time, from three to three and a half hours.

Fig Pudding.—*Ingredients:* ½ pound of dried figs, ¾ pound of bread crumbs, 6 ounces suet, 6 ounces sugar, 1 cup milk, ½ nutmeg, grated, 1 or 2 eggs. *Mode:* Mix the bread crumbs and minced suet, then the figs, chopped up, the sugar and nutmeg. Moisten with the milk and egg beaten together, put into a well-buttered mould, and boil on steam; serve with a sweet sauce. Time, from three to four hours.

Leg of Pork to Roast.—Choose a firm leg of about 8 pounds weight, scald and score it without cutting into the fat.

Insert a sharp, thin-bladed knife into the knuckle end close to the bone. Let it run along the bone nearly through the leg, work it round to detach the meat, so as to form an opening. Fill this with a stuffing of sage, onions, and bread crumbs. While roasting, cover with oiled paper until almost done, then remove, so that the crackling may brown and crisp. To roast, allow twenty minutes to the pound.

Sponge Tart.—*Ingredients:* Some stale sponge cake, jam, 1 egg, a little butter, 2 ounces sugar, 2 ounces flour, flavouring, milk. *Mode:* Butter a shallow pie-dish, or a deep enamel plate, cover the bottom with a layer of the cake, put a thin layer of jam over. Beat the egg in a basin with the sugar, butter, flour, and a little milk, add the flavouring, place this over the jam, and bake in a quick oven.

Indian Fritters.—*Ingredients:* 3 tablespoonfuls sifted flour, yolks of 4 eggs, whites of 2, marmalade. *Mode:* Put the sifted flour into a basin, and pour over it enough boiling water to make a stiff paste, beat well and avoid lumps, leave till cool, and then break into the paste the yolks of the eggs, beat well with a wooden spoon, whisk the two whites and stir them in. Have ready some boiling fat in a deep pan, and drop the batter in a tablespoonful at a time; fry a pale brown, and between each fritter put a spoonful of marmalade.

Baked Custard.—*Ingredients:* 3 eggs, sugar, 1 pint milk, nutmeg, puff paste. *Mode:* First line a pie-dish with

puff paste. Beat up the eggs, sweeten, and add the milk.
Pour into the pie-dish, and bake in a slow oven.

German Sauce.— *Ingredients :* 2 eggs, sugar, 1 glass
wine. *Mode :* Beat up 2 eggs, a little sugar, and a glass of
wine together. Put into a saucepan near the fire, and whisk
till it becomes a stiff froth.

Biscuit Pudding.—*Ingredients :* Some sweet biscuits,
sponge cake, and ratafias ; 3 eggs, nearly 1 pint of milk,
sugar, 1 glass of brandy, sultanas. *Mode :* Butter a pudding
basin and press into the butter some sultanas or stoned
raisins, then put in the biscuits, the sponge cake, and ratafias,
until the mould is full. Make a custard with the eggs, milk
and sugar to taste. Pour the brandy over first, then pour in
the custard, and steam one hour.

Plain Fruit Pudding.—*Ingredients :* 4 ounces each of
bread crumbs, flour, suet, sugar, currants, and sultanas, 4
eggs. *Mode :* Mix the dry ingredients together, moisten
with the well-beaten eggs, put into a buttered mould and
boil. Serve with wine sauce. Time, three hours.

Apple Sauce.—*Ingredients :* 6 apples, rind and juice of
1 lemon, 3 cloves, half a cup water. *Mode :* Peel, quarter,
and core the apples. Put into a stewpan with half a cup of
water, a little lemon-peel, and the cloves. When reduced to
a pulp, take out the rind and mash up with the juice of the
lemon. Serve in a tureen with roast goose and roast pork.

Apples with Dates.—*Ingredients :* Apples, ½ pound
dates, rind and juice of 1 lemon, sugar, bread crumbs,
butter. *Mode :* Choose large apples all the same size, scoop
out the cores and pare them. Stone the dates, and fill up the
centres of the apples with them and some sugar. Place in a
deep dish, grate the lemon rind over, and cover thickly with
bread crumbs. Squeeze the juice of a lemon over, put lumps
of butter on each apple, pour in water, and bake slowly.
Serve with cream.

Countess Pudding.—*Ingredients :* 1 pint milk, ½ stick
cinnamon, a strip of lemon-peel, 2 tablespoonfuls arrowroot,
3 ounces sugar, 5 eggs, 1 ounce sweet almonds, 1 teaspoonful

vanilla essence, some candied peel. *Mode:* Put the milk into
a saucepan with the lemon rind and cinnamon, let it stand by
the fire for an hour, then remove the flavouring and stir in
the arrowroot (previously blended) and the sugar. Let simmer a few minutes, and remove to cool, then mix in gradually
the eggs, well beaten, the almonds, blanched and chopped, and
the vanilla. Butter a pudding basin and sprinkle with
candied peel chopped up small. Pour in the mixture and
steam one and a half hours. Serve with orange sauce.

Baked Cocoa-nut Pudding.—*Ingredients:* ½ pound of
grated cocoa-nut, 2 ounces butter, 2 ounces sugar, 5 eggs, 1
pint milk, 2 tablespoonfuls bread crumbs, 1 teaspoon vanilla
essence. *Mode:* Cook the cocoa-nut in the milk. Beat the
butter, sugar, and yolks of the eggs together, lift the milk
from the fire, and stir this into it, with the bread crumbs and
flavouring. Whip two of the whites to a froth, and add them
last, pour into a buttered pie-dish, and bake forty minutes.
Whip the remaining whites with 2 ounces of sugar, spread
over the pudding, and return to the oven to brown slightly.

Pear Mould.—*Ingredients:* Pears, sugar, cinnamon,
cloves, lemon rind, 1 ounce gelatine. *Mode:* Pare and cut
the pears into quarters (as many as will be required for your
mould). Stew them very slowly in just water enough to
cover them, 1 stick cinnamon, a few cloves, and sugar to
taste. Do not let them break. Wet a large mould and arrange
the fruit lightly in it. Then to the liquor in the stewpan
add a little lemon rind and the gelatine, previously swelled;
boil up for five minutes, and pour over the fruit. When firm
turn out, and serve with custard.

To Boil a Tongue.—Choose a thick tongue with a good
smooth skin, soak it a couple of hours, then put into a pan of
COLD water and bring very gradually to a boil; simmer
slowly for three hours. To remove the skin, plunge into cold
water for a minute or two, and it will peel off easily. If
necessary, cover with greased paper and place in the oven to
heat up again.

Celery Sauce.—*Ingredients:* The white heart of a head
of celery, 1 pint milk, 2 tablespoonfuls flour, a little nutmeg,

F

butter, 2 tablespoonfuls cream. *Mode:* Boil the celery in salted water till tender, drain in a sieve, and cut into small pieces, make a sauce by boiling the milk with a spoonful of butter, thicken with flour, add a dust of nutmeg, and stir in the celery; lastly, add the cream. Serve in a tureen with boiled fowl, etc., etc.

A Calf's Sweetbread (for an Invalid).—*Ingredients:* 1 sweetbread, 1 ounce butter, cup and a half of good white stock, a little cornflour. *Mode:* Steep in cold water for a couple of hours, wash well and put into boiling water for five minutes, then again into cold for twenty minutes, to banch it. Put the butter into a saucepan, and when melted put in the sweetbread. Let it get gradually hot and brown all over, then pour in the stock, and let it simmer one hour, remove the sweetbread on to a dish, thicken the gravy with a little cornflour, and pour it over. Serve while hot.

Fish Soufflés.—*Ingredients:* Two teaspoonfuls cornflour, 1 cup milk, a little butter, 2 eggs, pepper and salt, 1 teaspoonful anchovy sauce, 1 cupful of cooked fish, some parsley. *Mode:* Pick some cooked fish free from bones. Mix the cornflour smoothly with the milk, put into a saucepan with a teaspoonful of butter, and stir over the fire till it thickens. Beat the yolks of the eggs and stir them in, add pepper and salt and the sauce, mix the fish with a little milk and stir it in by degrees. Whisk the whites of the eggs to a stiff froth and beat them in quickly. Pour into a soufflé tin and bake in a quick oven twenty minutes, sprinkle some chopped parsley over it.

A Spanish Dish.—*Ingredients:* 3 ounces of butter, 2 small onions, 4 large tomatoes, ½ pound of lean bacon, 1 quart good stock or broth, 1 pound rice, salt and pepper, the green ends cut from a bundle of asparagus, grated cheese. *Mode:* Melt the butter in a stewpan, slice the onions and fry them a light brown. Skin and slice the tomatoes, and add them with the bacon cut into dice, fry all together a few minutes, then pour in the stock. Wash the rice and throw it in, add pepper and salt, and let it simmer half an hour, stirring now and then, to prevent burning. Cut the asparagus ends up and add them, and if too thick, add more stock. Send to table very hot, and with a dish of grated cheese and a tureen of good gravy.

A Dish of Spinach.—*Ingredients :* Some spinach, 2 ounces butter, pepper and salt, and a dust of nutmeg, 1 tablespoonful cream, 1 egg, and a little milk. *Mode :* Well wash and boil the spinach till the leaves are soft, then drain all the water away and return the spinach to the saucepan with the butter and seasoning. Stir it over the fire with a wooden spoon, and when quite hot add the cream, and the egg well beaten up with a tablespoonful of milk. Serve with toast or without, according to taste.

A Rhubarb Trifle.—*Ingredients :* Some stale sponge cake, 1 bundle of rhubarb, 3 eggs, 1 cup cream, sugar, some lemon rind, some milk. *Mode :* Boil down some rhubarb in a little water with sugar, and the rind of half a lemon, grated ; crumble some sponge cake into a glass dish and pour the cream over. Make a custard with 2 or 3 eggs and 1 cup of milk, sweeten it and flavour with any essence preferred. Pour the rhubarb into the dish and then the boiled custard over all, grate a little nutmeg over, and stand in the ice chest, to get cold.

A Scotch Dish.—*Ingredients :* ½ a pound oatmeal, 1½ pints boiling water, salt, pepper, ½ teaspoonful mixed herbs, ½ teaspoon sugar, a little grated lemon rind, 1 onion, ½ pound cold meat (minced), 2 slices bacon, a little butter. *Mode :* Pour the boiling water on to the oatmeal, put into a saucepan and boil fiften minutes. Then add salt and pepper, herbs, sugar, and lemon, the onion cut up small. Mince the meat and bacon, stir into the oatmeal, and turn the whole into a greased pie-dish ; put some pieces of butter here and there, and bake in a moderate oven one hour and a half. Serve with good gravy.

Stewed Kidneys.—*Ingredients :* Some sheeps' kidneys, butter, pepper, salt, a little flour, a cup of stock or broth, 1 glass sherry, some minced parsley, 1 spoonful Worcester sauce. ⸱ *Mode :* Skin and par-boil the kidneys, cut them in slices and toss in a saucepan with butter, add seasoning to taste, and a slight dredging of flour ; moisten with the stock and add the sherry, parsley, and sauce ; let the whole simmer for a few minutes, and then serve with snippets of toast.

Rhubarb Jelly.—*Ingredients :* 6 pounds of rhubarb, sugar, lemons. *Mode :* Wipe clean, but do not peel the rhubarb. Cut it into inch lengths, and put into a large jar with about 1 cup of water ; tie something over the jar and stand it in a saucepan of boiling water over the fire, to draw the juice out. Pour off the latter and strain through a jelly bag, and to each pint of juice allow 1 pound of sugar, and the juice of $\frac{1}{2}$ a lemon ; boil for half an hour (stirring all the time), or till it jells. Pour into jars and store.

Bacon Curing.—There is much diversity of opinion about bacon curing, and I don't know that it is quite safe for the writer of a cookery book to offer advice. However, having some slight experience in the matter, I will merely offer it for the benefit of those of my readers who have none.

In the first place, after killing the hog, it must hang at least twenty-four hours to stiffen, then it can be cut up into two neat hams and two flitches. Take out the backbone by sawing down the middle and across the end of the ribs holding the saw or knife, both will be required, at an angle. The ribs can be removed or not, as preferred.

Trim the hams and sprinkle the whole four pieces liberally with salt, and let them lie some hours for the blood to run out. Then mix the following ingredients :—$2\frac{1}{2}$ pounds coarse salt, $1\frac{1}{2}$ pounds coarse sugar, 6 ounces saltpetre, pounded. Lay one of the flitches on a table and rub a quarter of the mixture well into it ; lay the second flitch on top, and proceed in the same way, rubbing well with the hand into every crack ; do the hams in the same way, laying the inside uppermost ; and have plenty of the mixture sprinkled over. It should lie like this for three weeks, turning it every other day, putting the top flitch to the bottom, and adding a little fresh salt to make up for the brine that runs off. Then hang in the smoke of a kitchen chimney for ten days or a fortnight.

I have found this simple process the very best, and far before many others that are a great deal more trouble. For years I followed this plan, and never knew it unsuccessful. It is, I believe, an English method.

Pine apple Salad.—*Ingredients:* 1 English pine, sugar, 1 lemon, nutmeg, 2 glasses sherry, or some colonial wine, a little salt, whipped cream. *Mode:* Slice the pine and drain off the juice, squeeze the juice of a lemon and grate some of the rind over it, make a strong syrup by boiling together 2 cups sugar to 1 of water; when cool add the juice from the pine and the wine, grate some nutmeg into it, and when cold pour over the pine. Let it stand an hour or two, and serve with cream.

Orange Salad.—*Ingredients:* 3 large oranges, 3 mandarines, 1 lemon, 1 glass of pale brandy, nutmeg, sugar. *Mode:* Make a strong syrup by boiling 2 cups sugar to 1 of water; let it stand by to cool. Slice the oranges, mandarines, and the lemon, and grate a little of the lemon-peel over the whole. Pour in the brandy, grate the nutmeg over, and, lastly, pour in the syrup. Stand on ice for an hour, and then serve with whipped cream.

Fruit Salad.—*Ingredients:* Any ripe fruit, sliced, sugar, nutmeg, 1 glass port wine, 1 teaspoonful spirit, 2 eggs, 1 cup milk, vanilla essence. *Mode:* Slice the fruit and lay it in a deep glass dish, sprinkle over it sugar to taste and a little nutmeg, also 1 glass of wine, and a tiny drop of spirit if liked; let it stand for half an hour, and meantime make a boiled custard of the 2 eggs and cup of milk, flavour with vanilla, and when cold pour over the fruit.

Anchovy Salad Dressing.—*Ingredients:* Yolks of 2 raw eggs, 1 teaspoonful of made mustard, 3 tablespoonfuls olive oil, 2 tablespoonfuls vinegar, 2 tablespoonfuls of anchovy paste or sauce, $\frac{1}{2}$ cup milk or cream. *Mode:* Mix the raw yolks with the made mustard, work the oil in drop by drop, also the vinegar. Add the anchovy sauce, and, lastly, while stirring, pour in the milk or cream.

Pour into the salad bowl and mix with the lettuce.

Potato Salad.—*Ingredients:* Boiled potatoes, salt, pepper, parsley, 1 small onion, oil, vinegar. *Mode:* Boil the potatoes

in their skins. When cold peel and slice very thin. Lay
them on a plate or dish, season with salt and pepper and
sprinkle with finely chopped parsley, and pour on to them oil
and vinegar in the proportions of 4 spoonfuls of oil to 3 of
vinegar. Slice the onion very fine and scatter it between the
slices of potato. Pickled eggs make a nice garnish for this dish.

Salad Dressing Without Oil.—*Ingredients:* Yolks of 2
hard eggs, 1 teaspoonful mustard, 1 teaspoonful sugar, 1
tablespoonful butter (oiled), 2 tablespoonfuls vinegar, milk
or cream. *Mode:* Mash up the yolks with the dry mustard
and sugar. Oil the butter in the oven, and stir it in till
the whole is in a thick paste, pour in the vinegar by
degrees, and add the milk or cream while stirring the whole
time. Always sprinkle salt over the salad before pouring in
the dressing.

Salad Dressing.—*Ingredients:* 2 eggs, 1 teaspoonful
mustard, 3 tablespoonfuls salad oil, 2 tablespoonfuls vinegar,
1 teaspoonful sugar, some milk or cream. *Mode:* Boil the
eggs hard, put the two yolks into a basin and mash them
with a spoon, add the dry mustard and sugar, then the oil by
degrees, and the vinegar; keep stirring, and pour in about
half a cup of sweet milk or cream. Pour this into the salad
bowl, and before serving mix the salad well with it.

Lobster Salad.—Choose a good fresh lobster, and get the
shopman to split it down the centre of the back for you.
Take out the fish and divide each half into two, three or four
pieces, according to the size of the lobster. Get the flesh out
of the claws and put it all on a plate in a mixture of vinegar,
pepper, and salt, whilst the other preparations are being
made. Now get a couple of crisp young lettuces with plenty
of heart, some endive, some mustard and cress, a small
cucumber, a little beetroot. Cut off the outer leaves from the
lettuce and endive, and wash them thoroughly in cold water
with the mustard and cress, and dry them in a clean cloth.
If the salad is very wet it may spoil a good dressing.

Next cut the beetroot (of course previously boiled) into thin
slices or dice. Cut the cucumber up also in either slices
or dice—there is no reason why cucumber should always be

sliced, it is easier to eat in dice-sized pieces. Next boil 2 or 3 eggs until hard, and throw them into cold water. All the ingredients are now prepared, and if wise you will have them close to your hand.

Now take a good-sized basin and begin to make the dressing, or mayonnaise. First of all, put in a teaspoonful of salt and half the quantity of pepper. These are put in first because if put in later, or after the oil has been added, it is apt to make the dressing lumpy. Break two eggs, separate the whites and yolks, and put the latter into the basin. Now with the bowl of a tablespoon mix slowly and steadily, stirring always the same way. When the yolks are well stirred measure out half a cup of the best salad or olive oil, and mix it with the yolks *drop by drop*, continuing to stir the whole time evenly and briskly. Everything depends on the way the oil and the yolks are blended, for if the stirring is stopped, or too much oil is poured in, the dressing will at once become lumpy, whereas if it is carefully and gradually dropped in the mixture will thicken and become more of a paste. In very hot weather it is advisable to stand the basin on ice, as it will keep liquid through the heat sometimes. Having mixed in all the oil add by degrees 1 tablespoonful of vinegar and 2 tablespoonfuls of thick cream.

Now shred the lettuce as finely as possible, using only the bleached or heart leaves; but keep one lettuce entire, for ornamenting the salad. Throw the shredded lettuce into a salad bowl, sprinkle salt over it, add the beetroot, the endive, cut fine, the mustard and cress, and the cucumber. Cut the other lettuce into quarters, or smaller if liked, and arrange the pieces round the bowl, slice the hard eggs and use them also for ornamenting; lastly, mix in the lobster, and the salad is ready to serve with the dressing in a sauce boat.

Some people prefer the sauce, or dressing, mixed up with the salad: it is all a matter of taste, but a mayonnaise sauce, such as I have just given, is best served in a boat and each person allowed to help himself.

Tomato Jam (**very good**).—*Ingredients:* 12 pounds ripe tomatoes, water to cover them, 6 pounds sugar, 6 ripe apples, 1 wine-glass essence of pineapple. *Mode:* Cut the tomatoes in quarters, and squeeze all juice and seeds out; then boil in enough water to cover them till tender; add the sugar, and the apples, peeled, cored, and cut up. Boil all in an enamel pan for one hour; when nearly cold add the essence, stir well, and when cold put in jars and tie down.

Gooseberry Jelly. — Choose ripe, sound gooseberries. Pick them over and put into the preserving pan, and simmer gently until they yield their juice readily. Strain through a strainer and again through a jelly bag, but on no account squeeze the fruit. Measure the juice, boil it fast for ten minutes or a quarter of an hour, and then add 3 cups of sugar to every 4 cups of juice (or 3 pints to 4 pints). When the sugar is dissolved boil together for about ten minutes, or till it jells on a cold plate, then pour into jars and cover securely.

Orange Marmalade.—Choose oranges with the best and cleanest skins. Ten will make a sufficient quantity for a small family. Cut them into quarters, and then with a very sharp knife shred them as finely as possible, cutting skin, fruit, and all; leave out any hard pieces. Throw this all into a large washhand basin, or a large milk dish will do, and pour over it cold water in the proportions of a cupful for each orange. If the large poor man's orange is used two cupfuls will not be too much.

Let this stand twenty-four hours, then turn into the preserving pan and boil till quite tender. If the sugar is added before the fruit is soft it will become tough and leathery.

Allow 1 cup of sugar to each orange if large, a little less if the small Seville orange is used—though, as a matter of fact, the quantity of sugar is regulated by individual taste or the time the jam is required to keep. If it is needed to store for months less than pound to pound is unsafe.

Marmalade of Mandarine and Lemon.—Choose sound, ripe mandarines and the thick, rough-skinned lemon—in the proportions of 1 lemon to every 6 mandarines. Having wiped them, shred all with a sharp knife, removing all seeds. Throw this into a large basin and cover with cold water, 1 cup to each orange and lemon. Let these stand twenty-four hours, then put on to boil, and when tender stir in the sugar, allowing nearly a cupful to each fruit—or less if not required to keep long. Boil slowly after the sugar is added, and when quite clear it is done.

This marmalade is improved by the addition of a citron.

About Preserving.—Jam-making is almost an art in itself, apart from general cookery. And you frequently find a lady who is no cook as regards culinary matters in general particularly clever at all sorts of preserving. I think everything depends upon the eye—a quickness in seeing when the preserve is done. There are some people who are always undecided, and will call in every member of the household to say if they think it is cooked enough ; while others seem to know instinctively when to take the pan off.

Another much-vexed point is the amount of sugar to be used.

This depends, first, on the climate ; secondly, on individual taste. In North Queensland it is seldom safe to use less than pound to pound, unless the jam is for immediate use, as fermentation sets up often within a week of making in the hot weather, and it has to be re-boiled.

Properly made preserve should never require re-boiling ; but the fault with most is that they boil too quickly. The best preserves are made very, very slowly, and with some fruit it is wise to boil it before adding the sugar ; others must have the sugar put on them over night, or twelve hours before making, to draw the juice from them. Where water is used to make syrup or juice it should also be put on the fruit some hours beforehand.

In making marmalade from small oranges 1 cup of water allowed to each orange is sufficient, but the large poor man's orange will take a pint to each. If it is required to extract some of the bitterness from the oranges they can be steeped in salt and water a couple of days before cutting up.

In making lemon marmalade a favourite way is to boil the lemons before cutting. This is old-fashioned, and not nearly so good a way as cutting them up beforehand.

In making jellies the fruit is generally boiled in water. There are a few fruits that make sufficient juice in themselves, but I much prefer boiling all in water.

For orange jelly use the small tangerine orange. It is

smaller than a mandarine, of a brighter colour, but not so small as a cumquat. It is too sour for eating, but makes the very best jelly, and with very little trouble. The fruit should be boiled slowly till it is reduced to pulp, then strained through a sieve first, and again through a jelly bag, then pint for pint of sugar added. For rosella jelly it is not necessary to pick the seed pods from the fruit. The best jelly I ever made was when, being in a hurry, I boiled the whole rosellas, just as they came from the tree, strained them carefully, and boiled with the sugar.

Citron jelly is one of the simplest to make and one of the prettiest for a table. To make the best jelly the fruit should not be quite ripe—there is more glutine in it then.

Stuffed Tomatoes.—*Ingredients :* Tomatoes, 1 cup bread crumbs, 1 small lemon, 1 clove, garlic, 1 onion, 1 stalk celery, two or three sprigs parsley, 1 tablespoonful butter, a pinch of mace, salt, pepper, and 1 egg. *Mode :* Cut a piece from the top of each tomato, and with the handle of a small spoon scoop out the inside, leaving a good firm wall, so they will stand up. Put the scooped-out pulp into a basin, and mix in the bread crumbs and the other ingredients. When all mixed fill the tomatoes, put on the little covers, and bake for twenty minutes to half an hour. Serve with a sauce made by heating in a stewpan the remains of the stuffing left in the basin. Add a tablespoonful of extract of beef dissolved in 1 cup of water. Let this boil for half an hour, then strain through a strainer on to the dish the tomatoes are to be served on, stick a sprig of parsley in the top of each tomato, and stand in a cool place till required. The sauce will form a jelly in the bottom of the dish.

Spanish Omelet.—*Ingredients :* 1 large tomato, 1 green chili, ½ an onion, 2 sprigs parsley, a bit of celery. *Mode :* Chop very small the tomato, chili, onion, parsley and celery, and pour into a stewpan. Stand over the fire till heated through, and then stir into the omelet as soon as it is put into the pan.

Omelet Soufflé.—*Ingredients :* 6 eggs, 4 tablespoonfuls powdered sugar, ½ teaspoonful vanilla flavouring. *Mode :*

Beat the eggs up well and add the sugar, stir till dissolved, and pour in 2 spoonfuls of hot water. Beat to a stiff froth, put into a buttered pan or small cake-tin, smooth over the top with a knife, and put into a hot oven and bake quickly.

A good Breakfast Dish.—*Ingredients :* 1 pint milk, 1 tablespoonful butter, salt, and pepper, 1 large tablespoonful flour, some smoked beef or fish. *Mode :* Put the milk in a saucepan with the butter. Put it on the fire, and when it boils thicken with the flour. Shred the beef or fish very fine or cut into small pieces, and drop into the stewpan. Let the beef cook two or three minutes. Pour into a deep dish and serve at once.

Baked Apples.—*Ingredients :* Apples, sugar, and water. *Mode :* Scoop the cores and seeds out of 5 or 6 large apples without breaking or cutting them, fill the cavities with sugar, and put nearly a cup of sugar in the pan with them. Pour in some water. Put the pan into a slow oven, and bake two or three hours, basting the apples now and then, or turning them. When done remove each apple carefully on to a deep glass dish, and pour the syrup round or over them. Let them stand till quite cold. Serve with custard or cream.

About Omelets.—When making omelets the great secret is the possession of the right sort of pan. An experienced cook *may* be able to turn out an omelet from a frying-pan in ordinary use, but an amateur cannot. The pan must be perfectly clean, and never have been burnt. An enamel pan is the best sort, and every kitchen should have one specially for omelet making.

Always beat the eggs, yolks and whites, together, and to every egg when beaten allow a tablespoonful of hot water— that is, if three eggs are used three spoonfuls of hot water must be added. Have the pan on the fire, with the butter melted and hot (not browned). Then pour in the eggs, and stir continually with a fork or knife (a spoon is too heavy), so as to cook the whole as nearly as possible at the same time. It must be done quickly, and without removing the pan. Let it cook a minute or two without stirring, and when set run the knife round and under the omelet and fold it over so as to double it. Then take an oval dish in your other hand, and place it on the edge of the pan, and flop the omelet on to it. This is a plain omelet. All others are made by adding the different ingredients after the eggs are turned into the pan.

French Salad Dressing.—*Ingredients :* 3 eggs, ½ teaspoonful mustard (dry), ⅔ of a cup of the best salad oil, 1 tablespoonful vinegar. *Mode :* Break the yolks and whites separately, stir the yolks round with a fork, add the mustard, and stir till well mixed, then add the oil, a few drops at a time, and go on stirring till in a thick paste. Beat the whites to a froth and beat them into the paste, just before serving add the vinegar. Never put salt into the dressing, but season the salad with salt.

Sponge Drops.—*Ingredients :* 3 eggs, 1 cup sugar, 1 cup sifted flour, 1 teaspoonful cream of tartar, ½ teaspoonful soda, vanilla or lemon flavouring. *Mode :* Beat the eggs to a froth with the sugar, then stir in the sifted flour, in which the cream of tartar has been mixed, dissolve the soda in a little hot water and add it. Beat well for a few minutes, and flavour with vanilla. Butter tin trays or plates, and drop the mixture in spoonfuls upon them, about three inches apart. Bake in a quick oven, and serve with ice cream.

Chocolate Filling.—*Ingredients :* 1 cup powdered sugar, 4 large spoonfuls of grated chocolate, 2 eggs (whites only), vanilla essence. *Mode :* Whisk the whites of the eggs to a stiff froth and add the sugar by degrees, then the chocolate and a few drops of essence of vanilla. Beat all together for a few minutes. This makes a good filling for puffs and cakes.

Chicken Salad.—*Ingredients :* 1 cold chicken, 2 heads of white heart lettuce, olive oil, vinegar, a few capers, 3 eggs, 1 dozen olives, 2 lemons. *Mode :* Shred the lettuces fine, and cut the chicken up into small pieces, season with salt and pepper and some vinegar and oil, add a few capers. Boil the eggs hard, when cold take off the shells and cut into slices, take the pips out of a dozen olives, and use these with the egg, and slices of lemon to garnish the salad, which is to be served with a stiff mayonnaise dressing poured over it.

Chocolate Jelly.—*Ingredients :* 4 tablespoonfuls grated chocolate, ½ cup sugar, 1 teaspoonful vanilla essence, 1 ounce gelatine, 1 pint whipped cream. *Mode:* Boil the grated chocolate in one cup of water, add the sugar and vanilla. Soak the gelatine in cold water for half an hour, add it to the chocolate and boil a few minutes. Remove from the fire, and when cold mix in the cream. Pour into a mould, and pack in ice till firm.

Maraschino Pudding.—*Ingredients:* 10 eggs, 10 table-spoonfuls sugar, 1 large packet of gelatine (soaked in 1 cup of water), 1 wine-glassful of maraschino (or rum and the juice and peel of a lemon). *Mode:* Beat the yolks and whites of the eggs separately. Mix the yolks and the sugar together, and add the liqueur, or rum and lemon, dissolve the gelatine in boiling water and add it, stirring constantly, beat in the whites, and whisk the whole for some minutes. Pour into a mould, and stand in ice till set.

Tomato Chutney.—*Ingredients:* 1 peck of green toma-toes, 1 dozen good-sized onions, 1 dozen large green chillies, ½ pound mustard seed, 1 tablespoonful each of ground cloves, cinnamon, allspice, and mace, 1 gallon of vinegar, or not quite so much, 2 pounds sugar. *Mode:* Cut up the tomatoes, onions, and chillies into slices, put them into a jar, sprinkle some salt over, and let them stand in a cool place overnight. In the morning turn the whole into a preserving pan, and add the mustard seed, cloves, cinnamon, allspice, and mace with the vinegar, and, lastly, the sugar. Place the pan over the fire, and let it boil until tender, which will take some time. Then pour into stone jars and tie down. This pickle is excel-lent eaten with cold meat.

Prawns and Salad.—*Ingredients:* ¼ pound of good cheese, 1 teaspoonful made mustard, 1 tablespoonful salad oil, same of vinegar, 1 teaspoonful sugar, a little salt, and a dash of cayenne. *Mode:* Grate or pound the cheese, mix with it the mustard, oil, vinegar, sugar, salt, and the cayenne. Make it the consistency of cream with a little vinegar. Pour it over some finely shredded lettuce or endive, and place little heaps of peeled prawns all round the dish.

Tea Jelly.—*Ingredients:* 1 pint milk (boiling), 2 table-

spoonfuls of good tea, or 1 of green and 1 of black mixed, 2
ounces gelatine, 6 tablespoonfuls sugar, 4 eggs, 1 pint cream.
Mode: Pour the boiling milk over the tea, and let it stand five
or ten minutes, then strain through a cloth. Soak the gelatine in a little cold water till soft, and add it to the tea and
milk, with the sugar and the eggs, well beaten. Stir this
over the fire till nearly boiling, remove, and when cold and
beginning to thicken stir in the whipped cream. Pour into
a mould, and pack in ice for an hour or two.

Coffee Jelly.—*Ingredients:* 1 pint milk, 4 tablespoonfuls
good coffee, 2 ounces gelatine, 6 tablespoonfuls sugar, 4 eggs,
1 pint cream. *Mode:* Pour the milk (boiling) over the coffee
and the gelatine (previously soaked), cover, and let it stand a
few minutes, then strain through a napkin. Add the sugar
and the eggs, well beaten, put over the fire again, and stir till
nearly boiling. Remove, and when cold and beginning to
thicken stir in the whipped cream. Pour into a mould, and
pack in ice for an hour or two.

Pineapple Jelly.—*Ingredients:* 2 large English pineapples, 1 pound sugar, 1 pint water, 1 lemon, 2 ounces
gelatine, juice of 2 oranges. *Mode:* Peel and cut up the
2 pines, and mash it with a fork, or run it through the
mincing machine. Dissolve the sugar in 1 pint of cold
water, add the juice of 1 lemon and a little of the rind, grated.
Pour this over the pineapple, and let it stand for two hours.
Put the skins and cores on to boil in a saucepan with about a
pint of water, boil slowly for half an hour, and when cold
strain and add to the rest. Meantime, soak a packet of gelatine, then strain the syrup through muslin, or through a
napkin, add the gelatine, also the juice of 2 oranges. Let it
come to the boil, to dissolve all the gelatine, then strain again
into a mould, and place on ice to harden. If liked, the
mould can be filled with alternate layers of fruit and jelly.

Chilli Sauce.—*Ingredients:* Take about 18 tomatoes, 2
large onions, 3 or 4 green chillies, 1 cupful of brown sugar, 1½
pints good vinegar, 3 tablespoonfuls salt, 1 teaspoonful each
of ginger, allspice, mustard, nutmeg, cloves, and cinnamon.
Mode: Peel, slice, and drain the tomatoes, chop the chillies

and onions fine, and place in a stone jar. Stand it in a pan of boiling water, cook until tender, then add the other ingredients and cook another half-hour. Strain through a hair sieve, heat again and put into bottles, add a few drops of brandy in each bottle, and tie down.

Tripe and Tomatoes.—*Ingredients:* 1 pound of tripe, 2 onions, a few herbs, ½ pound of tomatoes, pepper, salt, flour. *Mode:* Cut up the onions, and fry with some herbs in good dripping or butter. When nicely browned stir in a little flour. Peel and cook the tomatoes, and when soft rub them through a sieve into the stewpan with the onion, etc. Cut the tripe into small pieces and add it, pepper and salt to taste, pour in about a cup of stock or water, and simmer altogether for an hour. When serving, place the tripe on a dish, boil up the liquor, thicken it, add a few drops of lemon juice, and strain over the tripe.

To Cook Small New Potatoes.—Par-boil them first in water. Then remove the skins, and have ready a deep pan filled with boiling lard or good dripping. Drop the potatoes in and let them brown, drain, and serve with chopped parsley scattered over them.

Horse-radish Vinegar.—Make 1 pint of vinegar very hot, and pour it on to 2 ounces of finely scraped horse-radish. Let it stand one week, then strain and pour on to some fresh horse-radish. Let this infuse for another week, then strain and bottle.

Eschalot Vinegar.—This is very good for salads. Heat 1 pint of vinegar, and pour it over a quantity of chopped-up eschalots. Let it stand a week, then strain and bottle for use.

To Pickle Onions.—Get the gardener to bring you the smallest unions of his crop for this purpose, and they must be done while fresh. Having peeled off the outer skin throw the onions into salt and water, and leave them three or four days, or till a thick scum rises on the surface of the water. Change it each day if necessary. Rinse the onions and let them lie in cold water, in which has been dissolved about a teaspoonful of alum, for a couple of hours. In the meantime boil up some vinegar with a few peppercorns, two or three bird's-eye chillies, and some whole spice and ginger. Strain when cool, and when the onions are in bottles pour over them. They are fit to use in a week.

Pickled Eschalots.—Get the largest bulbs possible and the ripest—that is, when the bulbs have spread and the tops dried down. Boil up some vinegar with any spices liked, pepper and ginger. Fill pickle bottles with the eschalots, and when the vinegar has been strained and is cold pour it on to them. Fit to use in a week.

Cauliflower Fried in Batter.—*Ingredients:* A boiled cauliflower, 2 eggs, milk, parsley, salt, pepper, flour, toast. *Mode:* Divide the cauliflower into flowerets, make a stiff batter with the eggs, milk, and flour, chop some parsley fine and add it with the seasoning. Have a deep pan of boiling fat ready; dip each floweret into the batter, and drop into the pan of boiling fat. Fry a delicate brown and serve cn toast.

Mincemeat.—*Ingredients:* 1 pound raisins (stoned), 1 pound currants, 1 pound cooked tongue (or undercut of sirloin), 1 pound apples, 1 pound candied-peel, and 1 pound moist sugar, two packets mixed spice, 1 tablespoonful salt. *Mode:* Clean and stone the fruit; then put every ingredient through the mincing machine; add the sugar, salt, spice, and enough brandy just to moisten. Line patty pans with puff paste, fill, cover, and bake.

Superior Plum Pudding.—*Ingredients:* Pounded biscuits 1 pound, bread crumbs 1 pound, raisins 1 pound, currants 1 pound, suet 1 pound, 9 eggs, 1 tablespoonful baking powder, $\frac{1}{2}$ pound sugar, $\frac{1}{2}$ pound candied-peel, 1 packet spice, 1 teaspoonful salt, 1 wine-glass of brandy, and a little water if necessary. *Mode:* Mix all the ingredients together dry, moisten with the eggs and brandy, and stir till everything is well mixed. Scald, rinse, and flour the cloth, and allow room for the pudding to swell. Time to boil, four to five hours.

Delicious Conserve.—*Ingredients:* 6 or 8 ripe peaches, 1 pound of sugar, 3 cloves, a few pieces of cinnamon, a little

candied peel, 2 glasses of port or colonial wine. *Mode:* Peel
and cut into slices the 6 peaches, and place them in a
shallow, earthenware dish, with the sugar, cloves, cinnamon,
candied-peel, and the wine poured over. Set in a moderate
oven for an hour; then, when cold, turn into a glass dish and
serve with boiled custard. Time to bake, one hour.

Bread Omelet.—*Ingredients:* 1 cup sweet milk, 1 cup
fine bread crumbs, a little salt and pepper, 2 eggs, a little
butter. *Mode:* Mix the bread crumbs and milk together,
season with salt and pepper, add two well-beaten eggs, and
beat all together for a few minutes; put some butter into a
frying-pan, and when it has melted pour in the omelet,
and let it cook slowly until it sets; loosen the edges with a
knife, and fold one half over the other. Put a hot plate (to
fit the pan) over, and turn the omelet on to it. Time to cook,
twenty minutes.

Potato Puffs.—*Ingredients:* Mashed potatoes, pepper, salt,
3 or 4 eggs, 1 tablespoonful butter, dripping to fry. *Mode:*
Mash 5 or 6 large potatoes very smoothly, add 1 tablespoonful of butter, and season with pepper and salt. Stir
in the yolks of 3 or 4 eggs, and the whites beaten to a stiff
froth, beat this mixture well, and drop in spoonfuls into
boiling fat. Fry very carefully so as not to break the puffs
before they set; drain on paper, and serve on a napkin. Time
to fry, about fifteen minutes.

White Sauce.—Melt 1 tablespoonful of butter in a small
saucepan, stir in 2 of flour (well sifted), mix well, and cook
over a slow fire for two or three minutes, then gradually thin
with milk till of the right consistency. Sometimes a spoonful of cream is added, or a couple of well-beaten eggs, according to the taste or fancy of the cook.

SAVOURIES.

Celery and Cheese.—*Ingredients:* Celery, milk, white
sauce, grated cheese, bread crumbs, butter, seasoning. *Mode:*
Cut some white celery into pieces about 3 inches long, and
stew in milk till tender. Make a white sauce of 1 ounce
butter and 1 ounce flour, stir over the fire till a smooth
paste, and then add a cup of milk, salt, and half a cup of

G

grated cheese; let it come to the boil. Place the celery on a deep dish and pour the sauce over; then thickly cover with grated cheese and bread crumbs, scatter a few pieces of butter over, and place in the oven to brown.

A Pretty Supper Dish.—*Ingredients:* 4 ounces of rosella jelly, 2 ounces sugar, 3 eggs (whites only). *Mode:* Put the jelly and sugar into a basin, and beat them together; then in a separate basin whisk the whites of the eggs to a stiff froth, add the jelly, and continue beating for half an hour, then turn into a glass dish.

College Puddings.—*Ingredients:* Bread crumbs, suet, sultanas, currants, spice, sugar, 2 eggs, milk, rind of a lemon. *Mode:* Take equal quantities of bread crumbs, minced suet, sultanas, and currants; rub these together, and add a little mixed spice and sugar. Moisten with 2 eggs, well beaten, and a little milk if required; grate in the rind of a lemon. When well mixed take about a tablespoonful in the hands, mould into a ball, rub over with egg, roll in flour, and fry in boiling lard or butter. Drain these balls, and serve piled one on the other on a napkin, very hot.

Vegetable-marrow Jam.—Peel the marrow, which should not be too ripe, take out the seeds, and cut into pieces an inch or so long; put them to steep in sugar and water over night. Make a strong syrup by boiling sugar and water together in the proportions of 2 pounds sugar to 1 pint of water. When this has boiled a quarter of an hour throw in the marrow, and let it boil in the syrup till quite clear (about an hour). When done add a little essence of lemon to flavour it. Put into jars, and tie down.

Marrow Soup.—*Ingredients:* 1 marrow, 1 tablespoonful sugar, 1 teaspoonful butter, a little nutmeg, salt, pepper, 2 slices toast, milk to thin it. *Mode:* Peel and cut the marrow up, boil and mash it, and add the sugar, butter, and seasoning; thin with milk to the consistence of porridge, and heat to boiling point. Cut the toast into fingers, lay in the tureen, and pour the soup over, and serve. Time to make, less than one hour.

Standing Pie.—Very few, even good cooks, succeed in

making a satisfactory standing pie. Consequently it is not often attempted at home, being more often ordered from the pastrycook's.

I have endeavoured here to give the directions in their minutest details, but would advise the beginner to try it two or three times for family consumption before doing so for any elaborate supper or luncheon party. Practice makes perfect in everything, and particularly in the making of a standing pie.

Ingredients for the Pastry: 1 pound flour, 3 ounces butter, 2 ounces suet (rendered), water, pepper, salt. *Mode:* Boil the butter, suet, and about 1 gill of water, and the seasoning together for a few minutes; stir this into the flour, using a spoon or fork, until it is cool enough to handle, then knead it well, and set aside till it is almost cool. Take three-quarters of this, mould it in a round ball, roll out till about half an inch thick. Flour the bottom and sides of a two-quart "Billy," or a cake-tin will do, lay the paste on the bottom and work it round and round the sides, pressing it closely with the fingers until quite smooth. Let it stand a few minutes, run a knife around the edge and slip the tin out. If the sides show any disposition to collapse it must be rolled out and blocked again. The cooler the paste the easier it is to mould the pie perfectly, but if too cold it is apt to crack.

Ingredients for filling Pie: 1 pound of veal, cut in small pieces, 1 slice of ham, also cut small. Stew this gently in a cupful of water for about one hour; when done season highly with pepper, salt, and a little mace. Put the meat into the pie, and roll out a bit of the remaining paste for a cover. Brush the edges with egg, to make it stick, and when it is on trim with a pair of scissors. Pinch the edge with the fingers into a fancy border. Roll out what paste remains and cut into stars, leaves, etc. Wash the pie over with beaten egg, and stick the ornaments over it. Let it stand some hours before baking, then wash the sides and top again with egg, and bake in a moderate oven. It should take about three-quarters of an hour. The gravy is added after the pie is baked.

For the Gravy: Boil a veal bone and a ham bone (well broken) in about 3 pints of water till it is reduced to nearly a pint, season to taste, and when almost cold strain it; make a small hole in the top of the pie, and pour in as much gravy as it will hold. When the pie is cold the gravy will be a firm, tasty jelly.

When serving the pie should rest on a doyley, and should be garnished with parsley, as it is always served cold, and is an excellent dish for supper, luncheon, or picnic.

Small Standing Pies.—*Ingredients for the Paste or Crust:* 4 ounces beef dripping, 1 gill water, 1 pound flour. Make exactly the same as for the large pie, but weigh the paste so as to have the pies of uniform size, allowing about 2 ounces of paste to each. Mould on anything suitable; a potato-masher is very good. The filling for the small pies can be made of any meat liked; the remains of a fowl or turkey is very good, and can be put in without being cooked again. An ounce of meat is sufficient for each pie. Cover and orna-ment; after standing a few hours bake, and then add the gravy as directed in the other recipe. These small pies can be eaten hot if liked.

Aspic Jelly.—*Ingredients:* Any clean stock can be used as a foundation, but if none is at hand, make it by boiling some veal bones with 2 calves' feet and a ham bone, 1 onion, a sprig or two of parsley, thyme and sage, 2 or 3 cloves, and 2 quarts of water; and boil slowly nearly four hours, or till it is reduced to about 1 quart. The boiling is everything in making aspic. Strain through muslin or flannel, and stand away to cool. When cold remove all fat from the top, break up and return to a clean enamel stewpan. Flavour with a glass of wine, 1 tablespoonful of lemon juice, season to taste, beat up the whites and shells of 2 eggs and stir them in. Now let it simmer gently for half an hour; strain again through a jelly bag, and set by to cool. When required to set round chicken, tongue, or any other meat, it must be heated over the fire and run into the mould hot. Made as above it will keep three days, even in a warm climate; but if required to keep longer, brandy or whisky must be substi-tuted for sherry.

Oyster Croquettes.—*Ingredients:* Oysters, flour, butter, 2 eggs, pepper, salt, nutmeg, bread crumbs, lard. *Mode:*

Chop some oysters up small that have been par-boiled ; make a white sauce with flour, butter, milk, and a little of the oyster liquor, season, and stir in the oysters. Let this stand by to cool, then roll into shape same as any other croquettes, dip in egg and bread crumbs, and fry in plenty of lard.

Brussels Sprouts.—Trim and thoroughly wash some young sprouts, throw them into some boiling salted water, let them cook for eight or nine minutes, remove them with a skimmer into a pan of cold water, drain them well, and re-heat them with white sauce or good melted butter, and serve.

Cauliflower au Gratin.—*Ingredients :* Some well-boiled cauliflowers, 3 or 4 slices of toast, butter, white sauce, bread crumbs (browned), a few sprigs of parsley for garnishing. *Mode:* Cut the toasted bread into convenient pieces, butter them and arrange in a deep dish. Upon each put two or three flowerets of cauliflower, and pour over them some good white sauce. Sprinkle bread crumbs, previously browned, in a little clarified butter over the whole, and garnish with parsley.

Cauliflower.—Cut away the stalk and outer leaves, and thoroughly rinse and trim the flowerets if necessary. Plunge into a saucepan of cold water, add a tablespoonful of salt and about 2 of vinegar (this will prevent the cauliflower from turning dark. Bring to a boil, skim if necessary, and continue boiling for half an hour. Try with a fork, and if done drain carefully, and serve with melted butter.

Rabbits en Poulette (an Entrée).—*Ingredients :* One or more rabbits, butter, flour, stock or water, herbs, spice, 1 onion, 1 carrot, seasoning, 2 eggs, milk. *Mode:* Cut the rabbit into convenient-sized pieces, and let them lie in tepid water for half an hour. Drain and dry them in a cloth ; toss them in a little butter over a slow fire, but do not let them brown. When the pieces are firm dredge some flour over them and cook a little longer. Now add by degrees a little stock or water till the meat is nearly covered ; put in a few herbs, spices, the carrot and onion, sliced thin, season with salt and pepper. When the meat is tender remove the pieces with a spoon or skimmer ; strain the sauce, and add the yolks of 2 eggs beaten up with a little milk to it, stir over the fire till it thickens slightly; arrange the pieces of rabbit upon a dish and pour the sauce over them.

This entrée may be garnished with green peas, grated carrots, etc.

Macaroni and Tomato with Cheese.—*Ingredients:* Boiled macaroni, 3 ounces butter, 2 ounces grated cheese, tomato sauce, ham paste, bread crumbs. *Mode:* Put the butter into a stewpan, and when melted throw in the macaroni and the grated cheese; 'toss this over the fire till thoroughly mixed; moisten with a little tomato sauce. When serving arrange the macaroni on a circular dish or deep plate, pour some sauce (thinned with warm water) over it, and fill the centre with grated cheese, or cheese and bread crumbs mixed, with a little ham paste, or a few slices of ham, chopped fine; put alternate layers of macaroni, cheese, etc., and lastly sprinkle a thin layer of bread crumbs over the top, a little butter here and there, and bake in a hot oven. Time to bake, fifteen to twenty minutes.

Jugged Wallaby.—*Ingredients:* 1 wallaby, some sweet herbs, 1 lemon, 1 large onion, some cloves, water, and 1 glass of wine. *Mode:* Cut the wallaby into convenient joints and place in a stone jar. Add to it a bunch of herbs, the rind of the lemon, the onion, stuck with cloves, pepper, salt, and about a cup of water. Tie the jar down so no steam can escape, place it in a large saucepan of water, or, better still, a boiler, and let it cook in this way for three or four hours. When done strain off the gravy, thicken and add the wine to it, and serve over the meat or in a tureen.

Aspic Jelly.—*Ingredients:* 1 knuckle bone of veal, 2 calves' feet, 1 knuckle bone of ham, 1 onion, a bunch of parsley, same of thyme and sage, 3 or 4 cloves, and 2 quarts of water. *Mode:* Boil the above ingredients together slowly for four or five hours; strain the liquid, which will have boiled down to about 1 quart. Let it cool and then take off all fat. Season with salt, pepper, and a pinch of mace. Add a tablespoonful of lemon juice and the whites of two eggs. Return to the stove and simmer gently for half an hour; strain through a jelly bag till perfectly clear. The addition of a glass of sherry before the second boiling will improve the flavour.

Aspic Chicken.—Prepare 1 quart of aspic. When it is almost cold pour a quarter of it into a mould; let this set. Put in a few slices of beetroot, pour in a little more jelly, and when that is set place the chicken, which has, of course, been cooked, removed from the bones, and cut into small pieces, in the mould, placing it loosely, so the jelly can run between it, and putting here and there a spray of green parsley. Pour in the remainder of the jelly, and when cold turn out and garnish with parsley and capsicums.

Custard Powder.—*Ingredients :* 1 pound of sago or rice flour (either will do), 1 pound ordinary wheat flour, a little turmeric, essential oil of almonds 1 drachm, essence of lemon 2 drachms. *Mode :* Mix the sago and wheat flour together ; add sufficient turmeric to colour a good cream or yellow, flavour with the oil of almonds and essence of lemon ; work all well together, and put into tins or bottles. *Keep dry.*

I give the above receipt, as doubtless many of my readers have bought custard powder and used it while wondering of what it is composed. There are other egg powders in the trade patented by the makers, but the above is as good as any, and as innocent of the real thing—eggs. When eggs are scarce many professional cooks will use one or two, and then make up with some thickening and a little saffron to get the desired colour.

Old Maid's Pudding.—*Ingredients :* 2 ounces bread crumbs, 2 ounces flour, 2 ounces grated apple, 2 ounces minced suet, 1 tablespoonful currants, 1 tablespoonful chopped candied-peel, 1 small teaspoonful baking-powder, 1 egg, and a little milk. *Mode :* Rub all the ingredients together dry, then mix with the egg and milk, and press into a well-greased mould, and boil or steam. Time, one hour to one and a half hours.

Pea Soup.—*Ingredients :* 1 pint split peas, 2 pounds shin of beef, a slice of lean bacon, 2 carrots, 2 turnips, 2 onions, 1 head of celery, salt and pepper, 1 quart water, and 1 quart stock, 1 sprig mint. *Mode :* Put the split peas, beef, bacon, vegetables, etc., down to boil early in the day. One hour before serving strain the soup off, and press the peas and vegetables through the colander; return it to the saucepan, and add a good sprig of mint, let it simmer till required, and serve with fried croûtons.   Time, from five to seven hours.

Aspic and Oysters.—*Ingredients:* Aspic jelly, oysters, 1 lemon, and pepper.   *Mode:* Pour about a cupful of jelly into a large shallow mould.   When cold lay on it some thin slices of lemon.   On these place a couple of dozen oysters, dust with pepper, add more slices of lemon, and fill up the mould with aspic.   When cold turn out and garnish with lettuce or parsley.

Aspic and Salad.—*Ingredients:* 1 quart of aspic jelly, 3 hard-boiled eggs, 1 beetroot, boiled, a few capers, and 1 boiled carrot, 1 head of lettuce, and some salad dressing.   *Mode:* Prepare the aspic; then get a large round cake-tin, and in the centre of it stand a smaller one with a weight on it, to keep it in place; pour a little of the aspic in a basin to set, and put one half of what remains in between the cake-tins. When it has set lay on it some circles of the whites of the eggs, some slices or rings of beetroot, a few capers, and slices of boiled carrot.   Fill up with the rest of the aspic, and set aside till it stiffens.   Turn it out when ready on to a large round dish, and fill the hole where the small tin was with nicely chosen lettuce leaves and heart, then either pour the dressing over or serve in a sauce-boat separately.

Mincemeat (quickly made).—*Ingredients:* Some scraps of pork fat, $\frac{1}{2}$ pound currants, $\frac{1}{2}$ pound raisins (stoned), $\frac{1}{2}$ pound grated apple, $\frac{1}{2}$ pound sugar, 1 packet mixed spice, the grated rind of 1 lemon, 1 wine-glass of brandy.   *Mode:* Crisp the scraps of fat in the pan, so as to take most of the lard from them, then chop finely, or else pass through the mincing machine, with the raisins and apples.   Mix in all the other ingredients, press into a jar, and pour the brandy over all, and stir to mix it through; tie down and put away for a day or two, when it will be ready for use.

Shoulder of Veal (stuffed).—*Ingredients:* A shoulder of veal, some veal stuffing, 5 or 6 small onions, 1 head of celery, 3 turnips, and a small bunch of herbs, salt and pepper.

Mode: Take out the bone and fill the cavity with stuffing, roll up the meat neatly and tie firmly with tape. Place in a saucepan, with just enough water to cover it, and simmer slowly. Prepare the vegetables and herbs and put in with the meat. To serve—remove the tape, strain some of the liquor, thicken it and season with pepper, salt and a little vinegar, and pour over the joint and vegetables, which can be arranged round. Time, three to four hours, according to size.

Coffee Biscuits.—*Ingredients :* ½ pound butter, 2 pounds flour. *Mode:* Warm the butter in as much milk as will make the 2 pounds of flour into a stiff paste. Beat it with a rolling-pin until it becomes perfectly smooth, roll it out thin, cut into biscuits with the top of a wine-glass, and bake for ten minutes in a quick oven. Time, ten or fifteen minutes.

Lemon Cheesing.—*Ingredients :* 2 large lemons, ½ pound sugar, ½ pound butter, 6 eggs, 5 tablespoonfuls cream. *Mode:* Grate the lemon-peel on to the sugar in a small saucepan ; add the butter, and as it melts over the fire stir it constantly. Beat up the eggs, and add them and the juice of the 2 lemons, strained. Stir in the cream, and let the mixture thicken over a slow fire. Line patty tins with puff paste ; fill with the cheesing, and bake in a quick oven.

Doughnuts.—*Ingredients :* 3 pounds flour, 1 pound butter, 1 pound sugar, a little spice, 6 eggs, and 4 tablespoonfuls of yeast, with milk to make it the consistence of dough. *Mode:* Rub the butter into the flour, add the spice and sugar. Beat the eggs up with the yeast and some milk, and stir into the flour till it is a stiff dough. Leave it to rise for four hours ; then make it up into nuts and work in a few currants. Have a deep pan or saucepan full of boiling lard ; throw them in, and cook till they are brown. Time, about ten minutes.

Milk Toast (a nice Breakfast for Children).—*Ingredients :* Toasted bread, 1 pint milk, 2 teaspoonfuls flour, a little cold water, salt and butter. *Mode:* Lay the toasted slices of bread on a dish. Boil the milk, mix the flour smoothly with a little water, and stir into the milk. Let it boil a minute, then add salt and the butter to it (a good tablespoonful will be enough), pour over the toast, let it stand a few minutes, then serve with sugar or jam, if liked.

A Nice Supper Dish.—*Ingredients:* The remains of any cold poultry, 2 or 3 slices of ham, 2 ounces butter, 2 ounces flour, ½ pint milk, 1 small onion, a dust of nutmeg, a little lemon-peel, 3 eggs, and some bread crumbs. *Mode:* Mince the cold fowl and ham together, season with pepper and salt and put on one side. Melt the butter in a pan, and stir in the flour, taking care it does not burn or get brown, have the milk (in which the onion has been) nearly boiling, and pour into the pan by degrees, stirring carefully till it is quite smooth, grate a little nutmeg in, also a little lemon-peel. When the sauce is nearly boiling stir in the eggs (well beaten), and stir till it thickens, but do not let it actually boil. Remove from the fire and stir in the minced fowl and ham, stir altogether, and leave it till quite cold. Then cut into neat pieces, roll each lightly in flour, dip in egg and bread crumbs, and fry a light brown in plenty of good fat. These may be served hot or cold, garnished with parsley.

Calf's Head with Sauce.—*Ingredients:* 1 calf's head (cooked), 1 tablespoonful salt, 2 tablespoonfuls butter, 2 of flour, 1 cupful and a half of stock, half a cup of strained tomatoes, a little pepper. *Mode:* Boil the head in salted water and let it get cold, then cut off in slices 1½ pounds of the meat. Melt the butter in a frying-pan, and when melted stir in the flour, and let it get slightly browned, draw the pan to one side, and gradually add the stock, stirring the whole time till all is smooth, then replace over the fire, and let the mixture boil up, now add the tomato, the slices of meat and seasoning, and cook a few minutes. Time, from ten to fifteen minutes.

Flour Pudding.—*Ingredients:* 2 ounces butter, 4 eggs, 4 tablespoonfuls flour, 2 tablespoonfuls sugar. *Mode:* Beat the butter to a cream and add the yolks of the eggs, beat in the flour and sugar, whip up the whites of the eggs and add them to the rest, mix all well together, and bake in a moderate oven. Time, from twenty to thirty minutes.

Puff Paste.—*Ingredients:* 1 pound flour, 1 pound butter (from which all water has been squeezed), juice of 1 lemon, a pinch of salt, and some *iced* water, if possible. *Mode:* Put the flour into a basin and rub in about one-fourth of the butter. Now make it into a smooth, firm paste with the lemon juice and iced water; don't have it too soft or too hard, but just to roll easily. Having mixed the paste roll it out thin, divide the butter into three portions, then lay one of these in little dabs over half the paste, fold the other half over it, and repeat till the butter is all used. Roll it several times in order to thoroughly incorporate the butter, then set it away in a cool place for some hours. It is an excellent plan to make the paste overnight, and let it stand in the ice box till morning. When ready to make up the paste be sure that the oven is very hot, as pastry needs a hotter oven than anything, and should be baked directly it is rolled out, as standing in a hot room softens and spoils it.

In cookery there is nothing so difficult to make successfully as puff paste. It is next to impossible to make it at all in hot weather, for no matter how firm the butter or how cold the water, the natural heat of the hands will render it so soft that to roll it will be a difficult matter, and to get it to "*puff*" will be more difficult still.

But in tolerably cool weather, with good materials and plenty of patience, there is no reason why the amateur cook should not succeed.

Banbury Puffs.—*Ingredients:* Puff paste, 1 tablespoonful butter, 2 of currants, 2 of sugar, 1 teaspoonful of candied-peel, chopped fine, the juice of $\frac{1}{2}$ a lemon, and a little spice. *Mode:* Roll out thin some puff paste, and cut into pieces two and a half inches square. Mix the butter, currants, sugar, candied-peel, and spice well together with the juice of the lemon. Lay 1 teaspoonful of this mixture on the pastry squares and fold the corners over to the centre. Brush with white of egg, and bake in a quick oven.

Lemon Cheesing (a small quantity).—*Ingredients:* 2 tablespoonfuls butter, 1 cup sugar, juice of 2 lemons, grated rind of 1 lemon, 3 eggs. *Mode:* Melt the butter in a small saucepan, stir in the sugar, the grated rind of the lemon, the juice, strained, lastly, the eggs, well beaten. Stir well until it thickens. Time, about fifteen minutes to make.

Batter for Fruit Fritters.—*Ingredients:* ½ pound flour, 1 ounce butter (melted), a little salt, and some warm milk, 2 eggs. *Mode:* Put the flour into a basin, stir in the butter and salt, and moisten with sufficient warm milk to make it the consistency of batter, or that will drop easily from a spoon. Stir this well, and then add the yolks of the eggs well beaten, and, lastly, the whites beaten to a stiff froth. This can be used for orange, pineapple, apple, and in fact any fruit fritters.

Ham Soufflés.—*Ingredients:* 4 ounces flour, 3 ounces butter, 1 cup milk, pepper, salt, 6 ounces cooked ham, minced fine, 4 eggs. *Mode:* Mix the flour with the milk smoothly, and pour into a saucepan, adding the butter, ham, pepper, and salt. Stir over the fire till the mixture leaves the sides clean. Then draw off the fire, add the yolks one at a time, breaking them in well, and, lastly, stir in the whites beaten to a stiff froth. Have ready some paper soufflé cases well oiled *outside*. Three parts fill each case as they will rise. Sprinkle some fine bread crumbs over the top, and bake in a moderate oven. Time, fifteen to twenty minutes.

Cleaning and Preparing Ground Game.—By ground game I mean wallaby, bandicoot, paddy-melon, iguana, etc., etc. There is no more distasteful office for a lady to have to do than this, and though my way may be no better than any other, I offer it for the sake of those inexperienced housewives who may have often thrown away good food rather than go through the ordeal of preparing it for cooking. In the first place, none of these animals should be hung up uncleaned ; like fish, they require to be cleaned at once.

About the skinning I need say little, as that is very simple, merely advising the use of a sharp penknife. Having skinned it, take a bucket of water, and with the wallaby, or whatever it may be, seek a place some short distance from house. I advise this on account of the strong smell, as well as the mess you thus avoid making in the kitchen. Make a cut from the neck to the vent, cut across where the inside is attached top and bottom, and then you can easily tear the whole of the inside out,

Plunge the carcass into the water, and wash it well, when it is ready to be taken back to the kitchen, and cut up on the meat board. A large wallaby or kangaroo requires to be dressed just the same as a sheep, but that work is usually done by the men folk of the household.

All Australian ground game has a strong peculiar flavour, which many people dislike. It can be done away with to a great extent by soaking in vinegar and water, or by burying for several hours.

I have frequently buried wallaby to advantage, as it makes it very tender. Merely wrap it in paper or a cloth, dig a hole three or four feet deep, put it in, and cover over again. Unless left ten or twelve hours it will do no good.

The iguana is little or no trouble to prepare, and the tail part is that most generally used. It should be skinned, par-boiled, and used for curry, or many Bushmen like it cooked on the ashes, particularly if the iguana be a young one. For my own part, I know of nothing we have in the Bush in the way of animal food that is so appetising as the tail of a young iguana cooked black's fashion on the ashes.

Orange Pudding.—*Ingredients:* 4 oranges, 2 eggs, 3 ounces sugar, 2 ounces bread crumbs, ½ pint milk, 1 tea-spoonful butter. *Mode:* Grate the rinds of the oranges on to the sugar in a basin, and add the yolks of the eggs. Heat the milk, pour it on to the bread crumbs, and cover till cold. Remove all pith from the oranges, and press out the fruit or pulp (if possible do not use a wire sieve, as it spoils the fruit), mix in with the sugar and yolks, and stir in the butter oiled, also the crumbs and milk. Whisk the whites of the eggs to a froth, and stir them in lightly. Put the mixture into a pie-dish, and bake in slow oven for half an hour. Remove, and on the top pile some white of egg, dredge lightly with sugar, and return to the oven for a few minutes till of a pale brown. Time, from half to three-quarters of an hour to bake, and ten minutes to brown.

Stuffed Onions.—To those who are fond of onions the following way of doing them is much approved. *Ingredients:* 5 or 6 onions, cold meat or poultry, herbs, salt, pepper, some good gravy, 1 carrot, 1 turnip, some small mushrooms. *Mode :* Peel and remove a part of the core from the onions, and cut them down in divisions like an orange to an inch or so of the bottom. Mince the cold meat or poultry, season it with herbs, and salt and pepper, and fill up the space in the onions, then tie each one with string, to prevent the mince from falling out, put them into boiling water, and boil for three-quarters of an hour. Remove carefully into another saucepan containing about a pint of good brown gravy, the carrot and turnip cut into strips, and some small mushrooms. In this let the onions stew gently till quite tender, and before serving cut away the string and thicken the gravy. Another way to do them is by putting each onion into a paste of flour and water when stuffed, and removing it before serving.

Devonshire Butter.—In the hot parts of Queensland, where it is almost impossible to make butter in the ordinary way, or at least without very great trouble, this mode is the best to follow.

Scald the milk and set as for Devonshire cream, and skim into a big basin, then with a tablespoon or two forks (held the prongs facing each other) beat the cream as you would eggs, and it will soon be converted into butter. Then wash and salt in the usual way, using very little of the latter, or you lose the peculiar flavour the butter made in this way has.

Devonshire Cream.—Strain 5 or 6 quarts of the richest of the milk into a clean milk tin, and set it away in a cool place for six or eight hours, or till the cream has risen freely. Then carry the tin as carefully and steadily as you can and set it on the top of the stove, but do not have too fierce a fire. Let the milk just come to a scald (not a boil on any account) ; it will take from thirty-five to fifty minutes perhaps, and when done the surface of the cream will be wrinkled ; and possibly the cream will break away from the sides of the pan all round. Now, with the same care and steadiness, carry the pan back where you had it before, and leave it another ten or twelve hours, or more if you see it is necessary. Then skim off the cream, which will, or should, come in a thick, solid sheet, so you could almost roll it up. For serving, it should be put into a deep glass dish or glass jam jar, and helped with a spoon.

With any stewed fruit it is delicious, or with fresh strawberries, bananas, peaches, etc. On oatmeal, porridge, and all kinds of blanc mange, it is excellent.

Chocolate Mould.—*Ingredients:* 1 small packet gelatine, 1 cupful cold water, 1 small tin of condensed milk, $\frac{3}{4}$ pint boiling water, $\frac{1}{2}$ pint milk, 2 or 3 cakes of chocolate, or 2 tablespoonfuls of cocoa, a few drops of vanilla essence. *Mode:* Put the gelatine to soak in 1 cup of cold water. Empty the condensed milk into a saucepan, and add nearly a pint of boiling water and $\frac{1}{2}$ a pint of milk, now stir in the gelatine (dissolved), and place the saucepan by the fire. Pour some boiling water over the chocolate, and when it melts drain off some of the water, and pour on a little hot milk, and make into a smooth paste, thin with more milk and add to the saucepan, boil for a few minutes, stirring all the time. Pour into a basin, and when nearly cold add the vanilla. Beat with a spoon till the mixture begins to stiffen, then pour into a wet mould. Time, about a quarter of an hour to boil.

Escalloped Fish.—*Ingredients:* 1 pint of salt fish, 1 onion, boiled tender, 1 pint of milk, 1 egg, 1 tablespoonful flour, some chopped celery, bread crumbs, a little butter. *Mode:* Pick 1 pint of salt fish and soak it in warm water for a while, boil and chop up 1 onion, and add it to 1 pint of milk, an egg, well beaten, thicken with flour and boil smooth.

Put a layer of the fish in a buttered dish, with a layer of the dressing and some chopped celery over it. On the last layer sprinkle the bread crumbs and some bits of butter. Bake half an hour.

Apple Fritters.—*Ingredients:* 3 or 4 good cooking apples, sugar, nutmeg, 2 tablespoonfuls wine, 3 eggs, and flour to make a batter with a little milk. *Mode:* Peel, core and slice the apples, and soak them in some wine. Grate nutmeg over them. Make a batter of the eggs, 2 tablespoonfuls of wine, some milk and sugar. Make two hours before using. Dip each slice in the batter and fry in butter.

Fricassed Eggs.—*Ingredients:* Eggs, some good gravy or stock, thyme, parsley, nutmeg and butter. *Mode:* Boil the eggs hard, and cut them into quarters. Make some gravy or stock boiling hot, put in the herbs, minced fine, a little grated nutmeg, and about a tablespoonful of butter, thicken with a teaspoonful of flour, if liked, season with salt and pepper, and serve garnished with hard-boiled egg.

Potato Cakes.—*Ingredients:* 1 pound mashed potatoes, 2 eggs, ½ pound butter, ½ pound sugar. *Mode:* Mash the potatoes as finely and as dry as possible, adding no milk to them. Beat up the eggs and add them, together with the butter and sugar, if liked ; some prefer a little salt in place of the sugar. Beat all together with a wooden spoon for fifteen or twenty minutes. Divide into cakes about an inch thick and bake. Time from half to three-quarters of an hour to bake.

Sliced Apple Pudding.—*Ingredients:* 6 or 7 good cooking apples, sugar, 4 eggs, 2 tablespoonfuls butter, ½ a cup of cream, 1 lemon, ½ teaspoonful baking-powder. *Mode:* Peel, core, and slice the apples into thin flakes, and half fill a dish with them, scattering sugar over and between the layers. Beat the yolks of the eggs with a little sugar and butter, and add ½ a cup of cream, the juice of the lemon, and the baking-powder. Beat all thoroughly together, and pour over the apples, and bake in a moderate oven. When cooked, whip up the whites of the eggs and arrange on the pudding. Time, three-quarters of an hour to bake.

Plum Pudding (**without eggs**).—*Ingredients:* 2 cups bread crumbs, 1 cup flour, 1 cup sugar, 1 packet mixed spice, 1 pound stoned raisins, not quite a cup of beef dripping, or ½ pound of finely minced suet, 2 teaspoonfuls baking-powder, ½ cup treacle, and a little milk. *Mode:* Mix all together dry, putting the baking-powder in with the flour. Then pour in the treacle and the milk on top of it, and stir till everything is well mixed. Boil in a well-greased mould or a cloth. Time, from two and a half to three hours.

Plain Cabinet Pudding.—*Ingredients:* Bread and butter, a handful of raisins (stoned), 3 eggs, 1 pint milk, 2 tablespoonfuls sugar, nutmeg. *Mode:* Cut the crusts off a few thin slices of bread and butter, and lay them in a basin, throw in the raisins, cut up the sugar, nutmeg grated. Beat up the eggs with the milk, and pour them over the bread and butter, etc. Put into a pudding basin, tie a cloth over, and boil. Time, from one to two hours.

Bread Sauce.—*Ingredients:* ¾ of a pint of milk, 1 cup of bread crumbs, 1 small onion, salt and pepper. *Mode:* Put the milk on to boil in a small saucepan with the onion, well scored across and across. When nearly boiling take out the onion, and stir in the bread crumbs by degrees. Let it boil a few minutes, and add salt and pepper, stir well, and do not let it get too thick. Time, about ten minutes.

Paste for Tarts.—*Ingredients:* 1 pound flour, ¼ pound lard, 3 ounces butter, water to mix with. *Mode:* Rub the lard into the flour (a teaspoonful of baking-powder can be added, if liked, and to ensure lightness). Mix into a paste with a little water, and roll out three or four times lightly, each time dotting bits of the butter over it till all is used up. Then roll together and leave the paste for half an hour before using.

Family Pudding.—*Ingredients:* 4 ounces flour, 3 ounces butter, rind of 1 small lemon, 3 ounces sugar, 4 eggs. *Mode:* Melt the butter and grate the rind of the lemon into it, add the sugar, and stir well. Beat the eggs to a froth and mix them in, and by degrees stir in the flour. Beat all together for a few minutes, and then pour into a buttered basin and boil or steam. Time, two to three hours.

Baked Custard Pudding.—*Ingredients:* 1½ pints milk (3 cups), the peel of 1 lemon, 4 eggs, 2 tablespoonfuls sugar, nutmeg. *Mode:* Put the milk into a clean saucepan with the thinly pared rind of the lemon; do not let it boil. Beat the eggs to a froth with the sugar, and when the milk is hot remove the lemon peel, and pour it on to the eggs, stirring well. Butter a pie-dish, pour the custard into it, and grate a little nutmeg over it, and bake. Time, about fifteen minutes.

Plain Suet Pudding.—*Ingredients:* 1 pound flour, ½ pound minced suet, 1 egg, 1 saltspoonful of salt, enough water

H

to make a stiff paste, 1 teaspoonful baking-powder. *Mode:* Rub the suet and flour together, add the salt and baking-powder. Beat up the egg with a little water, stir it into the flour and suet, and beat the mixture for ten minutes. Flour a pudding cloth, pour the paste into it, tie tightly, and plunge into boiling water. Time to boil, one and a half hours.

Batter Pudding (baked).—*Ingredients:* 3 or 4 eggs, 4 tablespoonfuls flour, nearly 1 quart of milk, 1 tablespoonful butter, 2 tablespoonfuls sugar, flavouring, and a little nutmeg. *Mode:* Beat the eggs with flour, and add by degrees the milk, the butter, melted, and sugar. Lastly stir in the flavouring, and grate the nutmeg over the top, after pouring into the pie-dish. Time, one hour to bake.

Carrot Pudding.—*Ingredients:* $\frac{3}{4}$ pound grated carrot, $\frac{1}{2}$ pound bread crumbs, $\frac{1}{4}$ pound stoned raisins, 2 tablespoonfuls flour, 4 ounces finely minced suet, $\frac{1}{2}$ a nutmeg, grated, 3 ounces of sugar, 3 eggs, a little milk, and 1 teaspoonful baking-powder. *Mode:* Mix all together with the eggs, well beaten, and a little milk to a stiff batter, then pour into a well-buttered mould and boil. Or, if liked, it can be put into a pie-dish and baked. Time to boil, one and a half hours; to bake, one hour.

Mrs. Lance's Pudding.—*Ingredients:* $\frac{1}{2}$ pound finely minced suet, $\frac{1}{2}$ pound bread crumbs, $\frac{1}{2}$ pound grated apple, $\frac{1}{2}$ pound sugar, the grated peel of 2 lemons and the juice, 1 nutmeg, grated, 1 teaspoonful of baking soda, 2 or 3 eggs. *Mode:* Rub all the above ingredients together dry (except the lemon juice, which keep till the last). Beat up the eggs and stir in; lastly, add the lemon juice, just before pouring into the mould. Time to boil, three hours.

Vermicelli Soup.—*Ingredients:* Any bones, remains of joints, or else part of a shin of beef, 1 turnip, 1 carrot, 1 large onion, salt, pepper, and about 5 pints of water. *Mode:* Put the meat on to boil, with the onion stuck with 4 or 5 cloves, the carrot and turnip cut up, and salt. Let the whole simmer slowly for six or seven hours, then strain out the vegetables and meat, and set the soup on one side till required for use. When cold all fat can be removed; and

when the soup is wanted add to it 3 or 4 ounces of vermicelli, and boil for twenty minutes, then serve. Time altogether, about eight hours.

Parsley Butter.—*Ingredients:* Parsley, butter, milk,
flour, and salt. *Mode:* Put on 1 cup of milk in a small
saucepan to boil. Blend 1 tablespoonful of flour with a little
cold milk, and when that in the saucepan is nearly boiling,
mix it in smoothly and let it just boil, stir in 1 tablespoonful of butter and a little salt, remove from the fire, and then
add 2 tablespoonfuls of parsley, chopped *very* fine. Time
to make it, seven minutes. To boil it, two minutes.

Raised Mutton Pies.—*Ingredients:* 2 pounds mutton,
neck part, 2 pounds flour, ¾ pound lard, herbs and seasoning, 1 egg, and about 1 cup of boiling water. *Mode:* Cut
the mutton into small pieces and put into a stewpan, with
pepper, salt, a teaspoonful of powdered sage, a dust of nutmeg, and a very little water. Let it stew slowly till nearly
done. Rub the lard into the flour, and mix into a stiff paste
with boiling water. Mould the shapes in a basin or tin,
taking care there are no cracks. Fill each shape with the
meat. Make a cover of paste, fit it on, and pinch the edges
together (first wetting them, to make them stick), make a
hole in the middle of each, brush over with egg, and bake a
nice brown in a steady oven. It is a good plan to pin a piece
of letter paper round each pie when put into the oven.
Time to bake, half an hour.

One Way to Cook a Rabbit.—*Ingredients:* 1 rabbit,
forcemeat, a few slices of bacon, oysters (or mushrooms), 3
eggs, seasoning. *Mode:* Cut the rabbit into nice pieces, and
lay them in a deep pie-dish, with forcemeat between them.
Strew the oysters and the eggs, hard-boiled and cut in
slices, over. Above this lay the slices of bacon, pour in
about half a cup of gravy or water, cover with a dish, and
bake in a slow oven. Time, one hour and a half.

Macaroni Cheese.—*Ingredients:* Naples macaroni, 1 ounce
of sifted flour, 3 ounces grated cheese, a little made mustard,
cayenne, butter, bread crumbs and salt. *Mode:* Break up
the macaroni, and boil first in salt water, and when nearly

cooked pour on milk, and let it simmer slowly till quite done. Turn into a well-greased pie-dish. Sift the flour over it gradually, then the cheese, the mustard, and cayenne. Stir all well together, and add the butter in little bits. Sift a thin layer of crumbs over the top, and brown lightly in the oven. Time, one hour to boil the macaroni, half an hour to bake it.

Excellent Wallaby Soup.—*Ingredients:* 1 wallaby, trimmings from a joint, or 1 pound of shin of beef, 2 carrots, 1 turnip, 1 head of celery, 2 onions, 6 cloves, 6 peppercorns, parsley, thyme, a blade of mace, salt. *Mode:* Skin and clean the wallaby, and soak for an hour in vinegar and water. Break the carcass into several pieces, and put them on to boil, with the vegetables, cut up, the herbs, spices, seasoning, and the trimmings, or shin of beef, in about a gallon of water. Boil slowly but steadily for five or six hours, skimming constantly. Then strain and rub the vegetables through a sieve, return them to the soup, and add a little good sauce and ketchup. Put a glass of colonial wine in the tureen, and pour the hot soup on to it, and serve.

A Good Pickle for Vegetables.—*Ingredients:* 1 gallon vinegar, 2 ounces curry powder or turmeric, 1 ounce garlic, 1 ounce mustard seed, 1 ounce ginger, ½ ounce capsicum. *Mode:* Boil all together. Skim well, and pour hot over the prepared vegetables.

Potato Eggs.—*Ingredients:* 6 or 7 boiled potatoes, 2 eggs, 1 tablespoonful butter, 1 small onion, a little parsley, pepper, salt, and bread crumbs. *Mode:* Mash the potatoes very smoothly, and add to them the egg, the butter, the onion, pounded, some chopped parsley, pepper and salt. Mix all well together, form into eggs, dip in egg and bread crumbs, and fry in plenty of good fat till a golden colour. Lay on paper to drain, and serve garnished with parsley.

Apple Jell.—*Ingredients:* 6 apples, ½ packet of isinglass, ½ cup water, 2 ounces sugar, 3 eggs, ½ a lemon. *Mode:* Pare, core, and boil the apples to a pulp, press through a sieve, soak the isinglass in water and mix with the pulp, add the sugar. Whisk the whites of the eggs to a froth, add some sugar, and the lemon rind, grated. Mix all together and pile on a glass dish. Decorate with red-currant jelly round it, and stand in a cool place or on ice for an hour.

A Swiss Pudding.—*Ingredients :* ¼ pound cheese, 2 eggs, 1 tablespoonful butter, ½ cup milk, and cayenne. *Mode :* Grate the cheese into a basin, add the butter, the milk, and eggs. Beat all together, then dust in a little cayenne and salt, if necessary. Warm in a saucepan and serve on toast.

Lobster or Crab Croquettes.—*Ingredients :* The flesh of 1 lobster or 2 crabs, pepper, salt, spice, cayenne, 1 teaspoonful butter, 1 tablespoonful flour, a little parsley, 3 eggs, and some fine bread crumbs. *Mode :* Mince the lobster or crab very fine, season with the salt, pepper, etc. Melt the piece of butter in a saucepan. Mix in the flour, and then the minced fish, the chopped parsley, and a little water or fish stock ; let it thicken, and then remove from the fire, and stir in the two eggs. Put it by now to get cold, and when nearly so shape into croquettes, dip in egg, and roll in very fine bread or biscuit crumbs. Let them stand an hour, and then fry in plenty of lard or good dripping.

To Pickle Red Cabbage.—This is one of the simplest pickles to make. Remove the outside leaves, and thoroughly wash the cabbage, then cut it in thin slices with a sharp knife. Pile on to a large dish or a pasteboard, and sprinkle liberally with salt. Put on some vinegar to boil, with such spices as you prefer and peppercorns. When boiled let it cool, and add cold vinegar to it sufficient to cover the cabbage. Let the cabbage lie for twenty-four hours, then pack into jars or bottles, pour the vinegar over, and tie down closely. A few drops of cochineal will improve the colour.

Cheese Pudding.—*Ingredients :* ½ pound cheese, ¼ pound bread crumbs, 2 ounces butter, 3 eggs, 1 cupful of milk in which ½ a teaspoonful of bicarbonate of soda has been dissolved. *Mode :* Cut the cheese into shreds or small pieces, and put it into a good-sized basin, add the bread crumbs and butter, make the milk hot, and pour it over. Beat up the yolks of the eggs, add salt and pepper to taste, and pour over the mixture. Cover with a plate, and stand by the fire or in a cool oven. Stir now and then till quite smooth, then add the whites of the eggs, well beaten. Pour the whole into a buttered pie-dish and bake. Time, from twenty to thirty minutes.

Cheese Paste.—*Ingredients:* ½ pint of milk, ¼ pound cheese, 1 ounce flour, 1 ounce butter, mustard, pepper, and salt to taste. *Mode:* Grate the cheese and mix it with the butter, flour, and seasoning, put it into a saucepan, and pour the milk over it. Boil till the cheese is all dissolved, stirring all the time, then turn the mixture into a basin or pie-dish, and as soon as it is cold it is ready for use. Makes excellent sandwiches, and can be used on bread instead of butter.

Baked Omelette.—*Ingredients:* ½ pound cheese, 1 pound potatoes (boiled and mashed), 1 egg, 1 ounce butter, and salt, pepper, and mustard to taste. *Mode:* Mix the mashed potatoes, grated cheese, egg, and butter together, season with the mustard, pepper, and salt. If too stiff add a little milk. Pour into a buttered dish, and bake until a light brown. Time, about fifteen minutes in a quick oven.

To Clean a Calf's Head.—First of all, powder the hair with resin, after soaking it in warm water for a few minutes. Then plunge it into scalding water, holding it by one ear, and carefully scrape off all the hair. Many cooks use the scalding water only, but the resin is a great help in removing the hair. Then take out the eyes, saw the head in halves lengthways, take the brains and tongue out. Half a calf's head is generally enough for a dish. Break the jawbone, remove the gums and teeth, and then lay the head in a panful of warm water to disgorge.

Potato Pie.—*Ingredients:* 2 large potatoes, 3 eggs, cup and a half of sugar, ½ cup of butter, the grated rind of 1 lemon, juice of 2, vanilla or orange flavouring. *Mode:* Boil and mash the potatoes, and mix in the butter, grated lemon, sugar, and eggs, well beaten. Mix all together, thoroughly season with the essence, and bake with an under crust or in tartlets. Time, about half an hour.

Rice, Apples, and Beetroot.—*Ingredients:* ½ pound of rice, 6 large apples, peeled and cored, 6 slices of well-cooked beetroot, sugar, 1 tablespoonful butter, and a few drops of essence of almonds. *Mode:* Boil the rice in equal parts of milk and water till quite soft. Cut the apples into nice slices, and put them into a stewpan with the beetroot and just water enough to prevent burning. Simmer gently till the apples are tender, then sweeten. Also sweeten the rice, and add the butter and essence. Turn on to a dish, leaving a space in the centre, into which pour the apples, and remove the beetroot. Time, an hour and a half.

Beef-tea for an Invalid.—*Ingredients:* 1 pound of lean, juicy beef, 1 pint of cold water. *Mode:* Cut the meat into very small pieces, removing every particle of fat. Put into a jar and pour the water over it. Let it stand till the water is red, then place the jar in a saucepan of boiling water, and allow it to simmer beside the fire. Time, the meat to stand one hour, to cook two hours.

Vegetable Goose.—*Ingredients:* Any broken bread or crusts, 1½ cups boiling milk, 4 onions (boiled tender), ¼ pound chopped suet, 1 teaspoonful powdered sage, 1 teaspoonful chopped parsley, 1 tablespoonful oatmeal, pepper and salt to taste, 2 eggs. *Mode:* Put the bread into a basin and pour the boiling milk over it, cover, and let it soak; then, when soft enough, beat smoothly with a fork, removing all hard pieces. Chop up the boiled onions and add them to the bread, with the suet, sage, parsley, oatmeal, and seasoning. Mix all thoroughly, add the eggs, well beaten, and a little more milk if necessary. Make it the consistency of batter. Put into a well-greased dripping tin, and bake for an hour. When one side is browned, turn it over and brown the other. When taken from the oven let it stand a minute or two, then cut into squares, and serve like Yorkshire pudding. Time, about one hour.

Cheese Omelet.—*Ingredients:* 2 teaspoonfuls grated cheese, 1 teaspoonful chopped parsley, 2 or 3 eggs. *Mode:* Beat the eggs thoroughly, mix in the parsley and the cheese, and season to taste. Melt a teaspoonful of butter in a small pan, and when hot pour in the mixture. Stir a second or two, then let it set. Fold over and slip on to a hot dish. Serve at once. Time, about seven minutes.

Oyster Fritters.—*Ingredients:* 2 dozen oysters, 3 eggs, ½ pint milk, and enough flour to make a stiff batter, seasoning, and a little chopped parsley. *Mode:* Make the batter with the eggs, milk, and some of the liquor from the oysters. Chop up the latter, and add them, with pepper, salt, and a little chopped parsley, to the batter. Fry in plenty of boiling lard, putting in a tablespoonful at a time.

Plain Fritters.—*Ingredients:* 4 eggs, 1 pint good milk, enough flour to make a light batter, 1 tablespoonful of sugar, a little grated lemon-peel, or a few drops of essence. *Mode:* Beat the eggs separately, the yolks from the whites, add the milk, the flour by degrees, the sugar, and lemon-peel. Beat well, and have ready a deep pan of boiling fat. Drop the batter in a tablespoonful at a time. When a nice brown remove to a dish, and serve with golden syrup. Time to cook, three minutes.

Apple Fritters.—*Ingredients:* Apples, a little brandy, sugar, and some batter. *Mode:* Peel, core, and slice the apples, dip each slice into the brandy, then into the batter, and fry in plenty of boiling fat.

Orange Fritters.—*Ingredients:* 3 or 4 ripe oranges, 1 cup of sugar, 3 tablespoonfuls of hot water, 4 eggs, 1 pint rich milk, enough flour to make a batter, plenty of good fat or lard. *Mode:* Peel the oranges and cut them into thick slices, take out the seeds, and lay the slices in a syrup made by boiling the sugar and 3 tablespoonfuls of water together till thick. When well coated dip them into the batter, and fry in a deep pan of boiling lard or good dripping. To make the batter, beat the eggs thoroughly, add the milk and the flour by degrees, till you have a light batter. A little sugar may be added, if liked. Serve with a sauce made by squeezing orange juice into the syrup and grating the rind of half an orange into it.

Chicken Croquettes.—*Ingredients:* 1 pound of boiled chicken, minced fine, ½ pint milk, ¼ pound butter, 2 table-spoonfuls flour, pepper and salt. *Mode:* Blend the flour with a little milk, and put the rest of the milk to heat. When scalded pour in the blended flour with the butter, salt, and pepper. When like thick cream mix in the chicken, and put on one side to become cold and stiff. Then make into twelve croquettes, roll in beaten egg, then in fine bread crumbs, and fry in plenty of lard or good dripping. Time, about two hours to prepare and cook.

Italian Pastry.—*Ingredients:* 4 ounces of flour, 1 tea-spoonful sugar, a pinch of salt, 2 ounces butter, 2 eggs, a few

drops of flavouring. *Mode:* **Mix** the flour, sugar, and pinch
of salt into a thin batter with water. Let it stand for half
an hour. Put the butter into a saucepan, and when it has
melted stir in the batter, and let it boil till a stiff paste, but
perfectly smooth. Cool slightly, and then beat in the eggs
and flavouring. Beat for a few minutes, and turn on to the
floured baking-board. Take a tablespoonful of this paste or
batter, shape it like an egg, and put into a moderate oven.
When half baked scoop a small spoonful out, and insert whatever sweet or cream you like, and close the opening with
some of the paste. Five minutes before they are done brush
them over with sweet milk. These may be fried in the same
way as doughnuts, if preferred. Time to bake, from thirty to
thirty-five minutes; to fry, about five minutes.

Short Crust.—*Ingredients:* 6 ounces of flour, a teaspoonful of sugar, 1 teaspoonful baking-powder, 3 ounces
butter, juice of $\frac{1}{2}$ of a lemon, 1 egg, and about $\frac{1}{2}$ cup of
warm water. *Mode:* Rub the butter, sugar, and flour to-
gether. Squeeze the lemon juice into the water, and beat up
the egg and add it. Then mix the paste into a soft dough.
Flour the board, and turn it on to it. Roll out as thin as
necessary, and use at once, as if too much handled it will be
hard and heavy. Bake in a quick oven. This paste is used
for fruit tarts, edging for milk puddings, etc.

Puff Paste.—*Ingredients:* Half a pound of flour (sifted),
1 small teaspoonful baking-powder, a pinch of salt, 1 teaspoonful of lemon juice, 5 ounces butter, cold water to mix
it. *Mode:* Mix the flour, salt, and baking-powder into a
stiff dough with cold water, to which has been added the
lemon juice. A knife is best for mixing. Turn it on to the
board, and roll out to about half an inch in thickness, doing
it evenly and straight before you. Have the butter quite
free from liquid, and divide it into three portions. Take one
portion and lay it in small pieces all over the paste. Now
fold it over, first dredging a little flour over the butter. Roll
out again, and distribute the second part of the butter. Fold,
as before, and then do it the third time, making the paste a
little thinner. This is not a very rich paste, but quite rich
enough for ordinary use, and most suitable for covering meat

or game pies, making sausage rolls, etc.   Put into a hot oven for the first fifteen minutes, then lower the heat.

Buttered Beans.—*Ingredients:* Some cooked French beans, 2 tablespoonfuls butter, 1 cup sweet milk (or cream, if possible), 3 eggs, seasoning.   *Mode:* Put the butter into a saucepan, and when melted throw in the beans and let them fry, but not enough to take colour, pour off the butter and substitute the milk, and let them simmer till this is reduced. Season with salt and nutmeg.   Beat up the eggs with a little more milk, or cream, stir them in, and add a teaspoonful of butter.   Serve with poached eggs or without.   Time, twenty minutes.

Scrambled Eggs with Tomato Purée.—*Ingredients:* 3 large tomatoes, 7 or 8 eggs, seasoning, some bread crumbs or croûtons.   *Mode:* Peel the tomatoes, chop them up, and pass through a sieve.   Warm, and season with pepper and salt.   Scramble the eggs in a saucepan, and when just thickening add the tomato purée.   Pour the whole into a deep dish, and serve with nicely browned croûtons, or surrounded with browned bread crumbs.   Time, about twenty minutes.

French Beans and Onions.—*Ingredients:* Some cooked French beans, 1 large spring onion, 3 slices of bacon, a tablespoonful of butter, seasoning, ½ pint of stock, ½ a lemon. *Mode:* Cut the onion into slices, and fry (without browning) in some butter.   Cut the bacon into dice, and fry that also.   Throw in about 2 pounds of cooked beans, and moisten with stock (from ½ a pint to a pint).   Season, and let it all simmer slowly for ten minutes.   Serve with poached or fried eggs, and garnish with lemon.   Time, about twenty minutes.

Curry Pasties.—*Ingredients:* Cold meat, seasoning, curry powder, mashed potatoes, 1 egg, some pastry, a little milk and butter.   *Mode:* Cut the meat up very fine, free from skin and gristle.   Season with pepper, salt, and curry powder.   Mash some potatoes, and moisten with an egg, a spoonful of butter, and pepper and salt.   Line some pastry cases with the potato, fill them with the meat, and cover with potato.   Brush with milk, and bake in a quick oven.

A Breakfast Dish.—*Ingredients:* Thin slices of cold meat and bacon, 1 teaspoonful mustard (dry), 1 tablespoonful good sauce (any will do), 1 tablespoonful chilli vinegar, a dust of cayenne, 1 tablespoonful lemon juice, and 2 tablespoonfuls claret, or any colonial wine. *Mode:* Cut the slices of meat and bacon, lay them in a pie-dish, the meat and bacon alternately. Make a sauce by mixing the other ingredients together, and, having first sprinkled the mustard throughout the meat, pour this sauce over it, and bake in a quick oven. Serve with mashed potatoes. Time, half an hour to bake.

Rice Cake.—*Ingredients:* ¼ pound of ground rice, ¼ pound self-raising flour, ¼ pound sugar, grated rind of ½ a lemon, ¼ pound butter, 3 eggs, 1 teaspoonful baking-powder. *Mode:* Mix the rice, flour, and sugar together, with the grated lemon rind. In a second basin beat the butter and yolks together, then gradually stir in the dry ingredients with the baking-powder, and beat all well. Whisk the whites to a stiff froth, and beat them in. Pour into a buttered tin, and bake in a moderate oven. Time, three-quarters of an hour.

Orange Jelly.—*Ingredients:* Four oranges, 1 lemon, ¾ pound loaf sugar, 1 ounce gelatine, 1 tablespoonful brandy, 1 tiny pinch of saffron, if needed. *Mode:* Soak the gelatine in 1 cup of cold water for twenty minutes. Squeeze the juice from the oranges into an enamel saucepan, also the lemon, and pare the rind of ½ a lemon very, very thin. Add the sugar and the gelatine when soaked, and pour on from the kettle a pint of boiling water, stirring well. Let it boil two or three minutes, then remove from the fire, add the spirit and saffron, and strain through a jelly bag.

King Fish (baked).—*Ingredients:* A 5 or 6-pound king fish, 1 cupful of fine bread crumbs, 4 ounces of minced suet, 1 tablespoonful chopped parsley, 1 teaspoonful sage, a tiny bit of lemon-peel, grated, 1 onion, parboiled, pepper, salt, and cayenne, juice of 1 lemon. *Mode:* When the fish is cleaned lay it in cold water a few minutes while preparing a stuffing of the above ingredients. Then, having wiped the fish dry, put in the stuffing and sew it up. Put it into a tin, and cover with good dripping, *or oil*, and bake it a nice brown in a hot oven. When sufficiently cooked remove to the dish, squeeze a little lemon juice over it, and keep warm till the gravy is ready to serve with it. To make the gravy pour away most of the fat from the pan, and add a tablespoonful of flour to the liquor that is left, 1 tablespoonful of fish sauce, a cupful of good brown gravy or stock coloured with browning. Season with pepper and salt. Let this thicken over the fire, and strain over the fish.

Rosella Jelly.—This is one of the easiest jellies of all to make, and there is no occasion to stone the rosellas for it, unless you purpose making jam of the refuse, which is really not worth the trouble. Put the fruit into the preserving pan, and allow about a cupful of water to every pound of rosellas, or if you have a large quantity a little more. For example : for 20 pounds of rosellas 14 or 15 pints would not be too much. Boil quickly till the fruit sinks, or, say, for nearly an hour. Then strain through muslin or flannel, and to every pint of juice allow a pint of sugar, and boil till it jells.

Rosella Jam.—Having picked the flesh or fruit from the seed pod, throw the former into the preserving pan with about a quart of water, or more if necessary. Put this over the fire, and when it boils stir well to prevent burning. Then allow 1 pound of sugar to 1 pound of fruit. Less can be used, but not if the jam is required to keep any time. Boil slowly till it thickens.

Rice Flour Biscuits.—*Ingredients :* 2 cups flour, 1 cup ground rice, 1 cup sugar, 3 tablespoonfuls marrow or butter, 1 teaspoonful lump ammonia, powdered and mixed in dry, 2 eggs, a little milk. *Mode :* Crush the ammonia and mix it with the flour, rub in the marrow, and then the other things. Mix into a stiff dough with the eggs and milk, roll out, cut with a wine-glass, and bake in a quick oven. Time, about ten minutes.

Ginger Nuts.—*Ingredients :* 1 pound flour, $\frac{1}{4}$ pound sugar, 2 tablespoonfuls butter, 2 tablespoonfuls ground ginger, 1 tablespoonful mixed spice, three parts of a cup of treacle, a lump of ammonia the size of small nut dissolved in nearly a cup of hot milk. *Mode :* Put the ammonia into the milk first of all, then mix the other ingredients together dry. Pour in the treacle and the milk and ammonia. Mix into a stiff dough, form into nuts, and bake in a quick oven. Time, about fifteen minutes.

INDEX.